COFFEE CHRONICLE

A publication of the Coffee County Historical Society
Manchester, Tennessee
Linda Winters

Slavery and Beyond

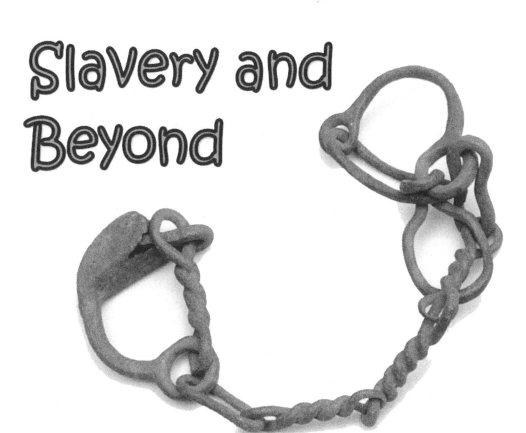

Coffee County Tennessee

February 2019   Volume 7, Number 1 $20.00

COFFEE CHRONICLE

February 2019   Volume 7, Number 1

Slavery and Beyond
Coffee County, Tennessee

Linda Winters, Publications Editor

A publication of the Coffee County Historical Society
101 West Fort Street, Box 2, Manchester, TN 37355
Phone: 931-728-0145   **Email: cchs1969@att.net**
Web Page: http://cctnhs.org/
Facebook: https://www.facebook.com/CCTNHS/

OFFICERS AND BOARD OF DIRECTORS

President.....................................Evans Baird
Vice-President........... ....Daniel Gregory
Immed. Past President   Joanna Lewis
Recording Secretary.......................... Pat Berges
Corresponding Secretary........... Patricia Anderson
Treasurer ....Linda Roper
AssistantTreasurer........   .. FrancesSimmons
Pubblications Editor................ ......Linda Winters
Director............................. Don Lee Anderson
Director.................................Larry McIntosh

- - - - - - - - -

Office Manager/Librarian ....Beverly Vetter
Museum Curator...Button Dale
Facebook Page Manager.................................Meagan Potts
Webpage Administrator..Cliff Baker

The **Coffee Chronicle** and bimonthly Newsletters are furnished to all members of the Coffee County Historical Society at the annual membership rate of $25 ($15 for electronic membership). Lifetime memberships are available for a one-time payment of $250.

Coffee County Historical Society meetings are held at 1:00 p.m. on the 2nd Tuesday of January, March, May, September and November in the offices of the Society located in the Historic 1871 Courthouse on the Square in Manchester, Tennessee. Our annual picnic is held on a Saturday in July at a location to be announced. The Board of Directors meets at 1:00 p.m. on the 2nd Saturday of February, April, June, August, October and December.

The CCHS office is open from 9:00 to 1:00 Tuesdays through Fridays with volunteers available to assist members and visitors with historical and genealogical research in our library and family files. Other hours available by appointment.
ISBN-13: 978-1798485859

Table of Contents

SLAVERY and BEYOND IN COFFEE COUNTY

THE BEGINNING

Slavery existed. As shameful a fact as it is, slavery played a major role in our American history. Until 1808, when Congress made the importation of slaves illegal, natives were captured in their African homelands, put in chains, and forced to endure inhuman passage aboard airless, disease-ridden ships to the American colonies. Those who survived the voyage then began a life of bondage.

Slavery was looked upon by many in the colonies as a normal, natural, and even necessary institution, especially in the South. Although Tennessee was not a large slaveholding state compared to others in the South (fewer than one family in five owned slaves in 1860), it had its prominent citizens who did own slaves. Andrew Jackson bought his first slave, a young woman, in 1788. By 1794 Jackson made part of his living in slave trading and ultimately owned about 160 slaves. James K. Polk was the owner of fifteen slaves. By 1841 Polk's plantation was troubled by slaves running away to nearby plantations, claiming mistreatment by the overseer.   Polk had the most recent two brought back and whipped.   Nathan Bedford Forrest amassed a fortune of about $1,500,000, as a slave trader and plantation owner before enlisting in the Confederate army. Joining the Ku Klux Klan shortly after the war, he was apparently one of its early leaders. Andrew Johnson bought his first slave, a manservant named Sam, in 1837. He eventually owned 8. Although the Confederates confiscated some of his slaves during the War, he said that many of them came back voluntarily after the War, and these he treated as freedmen. If he didn't free all of his slaves individually, he certainly freed them in 1864 when, as military governor of Tennessee, he proclaimed freedom for all slaves in the state.

The number of free Negroes in Tennessee had increased from 361 in 1801 to 4,555 in 1831. Free black men had the right to vote in the state until 1834 when Negro suffrage was abolished. Aside from the fact that the free Negro was permitted to attend private schools in Memphis and Nashville, to receive religious instruction, to sue and be sued, to make contracts and inherit property, and to enjoy legal marriage, no rights of citizenship remained to him after 1834. A sort of prisoner on parole, he was both socially and economically controlled.

Tennessee was a leading state in attempts to abolish slavery before 1830. In 1831, "defensive legislation" was enacted providing that, in Tennessee, emancipation could take place only on the condition of immediate deportation from the state. The American Colonization Society had established a colony on the west coast of Africa in 1922 that became known as the Independent Nation of Liberia, and removal of freed slaves to this location was advocated. In his will dated March 6, 1856, Elias Teal of Coffee County made the following stipulation: "...to my two children, Langston and Nancy Ann, all my real and personal property … …Should both of my children die before they become of age leaving no heirs of their body, I then desire and is my will that all my slaves to wit, Sarah, Bill, Jo, Jane, Peter, Tony, Clenton, Fannie, Martha, Mary, Mariah, Rebecca, Betsy and Hector be set free and sent to Liberia on the Coast of Africa and that all my property real and personal be sold and the proceeds thereof be used by my executors to remove said slaves as above named and that the balance of the funds over and above defraying their expenses be equally distributed among them by my said executors, share and share alike..." There were only 287 free Negroes sent to Liberia from TN from 1820-1866.

Free blacks in the state weren't allowed to associate with slaves, for fear they would encourage them to flee. The 1831 slave uprising of Nat Turner badly frightened slave owners, and by 1834 the tide began to turn against abolition because of growing concerns over slave rebellions and riots in neighboring states. Slave owners feared uprisings, and some increased their strength through vigilante action, a traditional method for handling slavery crises. In at least Coffee, Hickman, Maury, Montgomery, Shelby and Warren counties, civilian bands and Confederate Guerillas employed violence and terror in efforts to maintain slavery. The Underground Railroad saw an explosion of activity in the 1840s. In 1842, the Supreme Court ruled that states did not have to aid in the return of runaway slaves. This rule did not set well with slaveholders, and in an attempt to appease the South, Congress passed the Compromise of 1850, which contained the Fugitive Slave Act. The law gave slave owners the right to organize a posse at any point in the United States to aid in recapturing runaway slaves. This made it easy to seize and enslave any black man or woman at large, which put the free blacks in jeopardy. Courts, police, and private citizens everywhere in the United States were obligated to assist in the recapture of runaways. Furthermore, people who were caught helping slaves served jail time as well as paid fines and restitution to the slave owner. Handbills and newspaper advertisements offering rewards for runaway slaves became commonplace. The following two ads appeared in the July 7, 1860 edition of Manchester's newspaper, *The People's Paper*: "$10 REWARD. Ranaway from the Subscriber on the 1st inst., a Negro man named Sye, is about 22 years of age, five feet ten inches high, black complexion, full round face, and has very little to say. He was purchased by A. B. Robertson, of the estate of Rogers, deceased, and has been employed in the Manchester Mills for a considerable length of time, up to last spring. It is quite probable that he is in the vicinity of Manchester or Tullahoma. The above reward will be given for his delivery to me or in any jail so I can get him. J. J. PATTON." And: "$50 REWARD. Ranaway from the Subscriber near Shelbyville, Tenn., on the 18th day of April last, a Negro man named George, aged about 28 years, 6 feet 2 inches high, and weighs about 180 pounds and of black complexion. Said boy was sold in Manchester, Coffee County, on the 1st Monday in April last, as the property of James Jinkins, deceased. I will give FIFTY DOLLARS for the apprehension and confinement of said boy in any jail, so that I get him. Address WM. Little at Shelbyville. WM. LITTLE."

"Slaves are generally expected to sing as well as to work."
~~Frederick Douglass, "My Bondage and My Freedom"

SLAVERY AND THE CIVIL WAR

With the beginning of the Civil War, the stage was being set for the eradication of slavery. The controversy as to the cause of the War will go on as long as America stands. But whether it was slavery, secessionism, states' rights, economic and political differences, trade and tariff, or family and home, only a small percentage of southerners owned slaves and few Union soldiers would ever have admitted to fighting to free the Negroes. Each side fought the War in earnest for what they believed was a just cause.

When the war hit Tennessee, many blacks were able to flee their masters and join ranks with the Union forces. By 1863 the Army of Tennessee had opened a recruiting station in Tullahoma, and Secretary of War Edwin Stanton made it clear that "all Colored Troops will forever be free." By 1865, Tennessee had 20,133 Black Enlistees. Not all black soldiers willingly joined ranks with the Union. In many cases, slaves of Confederate owners were impressed into service, and were not paid wages, but were given food rations for themselves only. This created a hardship on slave families, and in time, Union authorities would be forced to issue food to the suffering families, though they would deny food to Confederate women and children. And, not all Negroes taken by the Union served as soldiers.

While settling the estate of John Cash of Coffee County in 1863, administrator J. F. L. Fares wrote, "I also report that the following Negroes belonging to said estate is now in the possession of the Federal Army of the United States as was prior to our administration, to wit: A woman named Sarah aged 40 years, a boy named Thomas aged 22 years, a boy Abe aged 19, George a boy 17 years, a boy Calvin 13 years, a boy Frank aged 6 years, a girl Susan 4 years, being seven in number."

The Union was not the only Army interested in enlisting black men. Confederate Major General Patrick Cleburne had been discussing a plan for freeing slaves and enrolling them in the Confederate forces. Some Confederates retaliated against their Unionist neighbors by seizing their slaves. Just after the end of the war, F. A.

Silvertooth of Coffee County was charged by the military authorities "of having gone to the home of J. J. Mankins and confiscated his nigras and took them to his house while Mankins was in the Union Army."

Several slaves were given employment with the Union at Pocahontas. In June of 1863, Lieutenant S. E. Adams of that place was unhappy when several he had employed were enticed away by a Colored Sergeant called Web to join the 2nd Alabama Regiment. Warren Hill, Jackson Foot, Andy Ayres, Sampson Harbin, Dany Moon, Tom Frazier, Andy Spell, Fitz Parmer and Isaac Connsel had drawn among them a total of 8 shirts, 7 pairs of socks, 8 pairs of shoes and 3 blouses for which the 2nd Brigade at Pocahontas was out the cost. At the end of July Lieutenant Adams filed another report listing the following persons hired by him, their occupations and wages:

Thomas Hooker	Laborer	$10 per month
Edgar Madlock	Laborer	$10
Henry Madlock	Laborer	$10
Charles Ray	Laborer	$10
George McGuff Ray	Laborer	$10
Willis Ray	Laborer	$10
Robert Ray	Laborer	$10
Philip Davy	Laborer	$10
John Alexander	Laborer	$10
Eva Ray	Cook for QM Employees	$ 5
Margaret Ray	Cook for Teamsters	$ 5
Harriet Cole	Cook for Contrabands	$ 5
Clemain Cole	Cook for Teamsters	$ 5

Gangs of bushwhackers and guerillas, out for personal gain and destruction, abounded during the War. With the arrival of the Union army in Tullahoma many black men and women had flocked into their camps, erected hundreds of rough shelters in and around the village, and secured employment in the Quartermaster Department as skilled teamsters, cooks and unskilled laborers. Near the end of the War when the U. S. Forces temporarily evacuated Tullahoma, terror, excitement, and anxiety struck the

Negroes being left behind. Guerillas came into town, robbed peaceable citizens and, in general, behaved in a "most shameful and cowardly manner more resembling savages." They were especially severe on the Negroes and took particular pains to burn every Negro cabin, house and shanty in town. Major General Robert Huston Milroy, born in Washington County, Indiana, and serving with the 9th Indiana Regiment, was an ardent abolitionist and bore a grudge against all individuals associated with slavery. Upon returning to Tullahoma in Dec. 1864, and finding the havoc wreaked by the guerillas during his absence, he began making an assessment of who was most able to pay, and ended up with a list of 84 names. Partly out of a sense of justice and partly out of a desire to humiliate those on the other side, the general decided to not only collect monetary recompense, but to also replace the housing of the Negroes. Milroy's list named 54 citizens who were to work on rebuilding the burned Negro homes, and 30 who were to furnish rations, tools, etc. The list was titled "The following named citizens are disloyal, and can be assessed for damages done by their Bushwhacking friends…"

On February 22, 1865 Tennessee passed a referendum abolishing slavery, and in spring of that year the War ended.

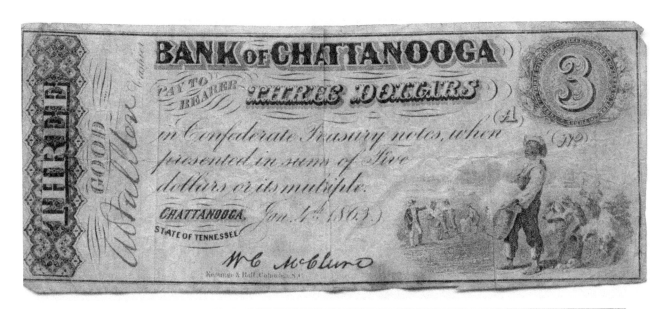

Bank of Chattanooga $3 Confederate note depicted Slaves Picking Cotton

SLAVERY AFTER THE WAR

Having lived in slavery all their lives, some had difficulty adjusting to their newly found freedom, and in many cases their new status required adjustments in actions and attitudes. A few slaves were so attached to paternalistic owners that they ignored their freedom for a time. Some agreed to stay with their masters until the crops were brought in or such a time as the master could do without them. Some freedmen remained with their old masters for life.

Near Hillsboro a farmer named C. F. Herd called for help in evicting "the colored man Ben Patton now living on the Patterson Place." When Herd seized the Patterson place to satisfy a debt, he found Patton living there even though he was not, and never had been, a slave of Patterson. Patton had no legal claim to the land, but refused to leave or to pay rent. Herd and Patton were able to settle their dispute outside of court.

In comparison to the number of blacks who lived through slavery, individual stories and information are virtually nonexistent. After obtaining their freedom, blacks seldom spoke of slavery. Reliving the shame and humiliation they had experienced was something they were unable to consider.

In the early 20th century, the Works Project Administration and Fisk University students interviewed former slaves who were at least 10 years old at the time the Civil War ended, endeavoring to collect oral histories. They did a notable job, and many stories otherwise lost were preserved. Although much of the information supplied by the aged former slaves is how they remembered or perceived things, it is certain that fear of retaliation or loss of a pension tainted some of the narratives. A slave might tell of beatings received, but then quickly add the disclaimer that "I deserved it" or "Marstar an Misses was kind to us."

Some of the WPA narratives collected on ex-slaves made mention of Coffee County: An 88-year-old unnamed man told how he had been sold 4 times in his life; the third time "I was sold to Dr. Whitson in Osceola. Dr. Whitson bought 10 of us in that drove and brought us from Osceola to Tullahoma, TN, in 1860, prior to the beginning of the Civil War." He goes on to say they were headed to Mississippi to be sold, but when they reached Stevenson, AL, a Ben Harris bought all 10 and brought them back to Nashville.

Ann Matthews, a slave born in Murfreesboro, tells how they received nothing when freedom was declared. Her daddy built a sapling house in the woods and left his children there. After two weeks without any food Ann stated, "I went up what iz called de nine mile cut near Tullahoma, and asked a woman if she would let us have some bread. She give me some meat and bread, and told me to come back. I went back home en we ate something, and I went back to the woman's house, she give me a sack of flour and a big piece of middlin' meat. We was scarred, being there 'lone so I would set up while my brothers slept, then I'd sleep in the daytime. One night somebody knocked at the door and it was my daddy and he had two sacks of food, and the other chilluns got up and we ate a big meal."

She also tells of the Ku Klux Klan in Manchester. They "wore big, high hats, red handkerchiefs on their faces, and red covers on their horses. They took two niggers out of jail and hung them from a chestnut tree."

Another ex-slave, Maggie Pinkard told how she was born in Nashville on the farm of Billie and Annie Robertson. Their daughter, Susan, "took me and mammy with her when she got married and moved on another big farm about three mile from the old master's plantation." During the Civil War, "the Yanks finally come to our place. After the master lost all his things, he left out for Coffee County, Tenn., where we stayed during the rest of the war. Sometimes though he took a bunch of the field hands down in Louisiana somewheres. One of the neighbors down in Coffee County made a wedding dress for my oldest sister when she married. It was a wool dress, but I don't remember what was its style. After the war they had big weddings. The parents fix up the wedding dinner. There was cakes two foot high! Pound cakes they was. Everything was pound cakes in them days. They was baked in the old time iron dutch oven."

A Coffee County, TN master worked on commission for his neighbors to carry "a bunch of field hands down in Louisiana" every year. Hamilton Brown earned a commission for arranging interstate sales for his neighbors. When prices were lower than he desired, he withheld the laborers for a better profit. In one instance, he advised the owner, "I think the opportunity will be much better for selling them in the fall. I have no doubt but I shall be able to sell for a much better price then than at this time."

While many slave masters may have been reluctant to separate slave families, such compassion was not always the case. Many slave families were destroyed by the masters' desire to maximize profits. The auction block and traveling speculators loomed like ever-present shadows, and slaves "lived in constant fear that they would be sold away from their families." Maggie Pinkard, former slave of Coffee County, expressively describes the recurrent trauma: "When the slaves got a feeling there was going to be an auction, they would pray. The night before the sale they would pray in their cabins. You could hear the hum of voices in all the cabins down the row."

There are various other references to slaves that deserve to be included in a history of Coffee County. These are included below.

Miss Christine Vaughan in her play "The Flood of Years" states: "A Mr. Reynolds dug the race and built the Hampton Mill in Hillsboro with slave labor. Over fifty slaves died of typhoid fever at that time."

-- Wiley Preston Shelton was a farmer who owned real estate worth $1200 and one slave in 1860.

--Lewis B. Morgan, lawyer and chairman of the county court, joined the pro-slavery party, and took up arms against John Brown and his supporters.

--Sometime between 1840 and 1860 the Rodes family of Richmond, VA received a land grant of 1000 acres near Summitville. In order to reach this land, the family and their 100 slaves traveled for six months by covered wagon.

--Mose Wooten, slave of Fannie Wooten, was said to have killed another man in her house. Mose lived to die of old age, and is buried in the Hickerson Cemetery on Powers Bridge Road.

--A law suit, (H. C. Norton vs. B. F. Moore) dated Dec. 17, 1859 was sent to the Supreme Court. The suit was brought to recover three negroes named Caroline, priced at $925, Clarissa, age 5, at $450, and Rufus, age 4, at $300. The bill of sale stated the slaves were sound and later events proved that they were not.

--On May 20, 1844, William S. Elkins sold to George N. Whitson for $250 his undivided interest in 4 slaves.

--Webb Thomas had been a slave and lived to be 100+ years old.

--Dr. T. P. Stephenson and his wife, Lucy, were noted throughout the county for their kindness to their Negro slaves.

--Peter J. Thomas freed all his slaves before the Civil War.

--In April 1837, John P. Hickerson wrote to his brother, Lytle, in Wilkesboro, NC, "Plenty of Negroes for sale in this county, but no buyers"

--Col. Massie Hill was a slave holder, and came from East Tennessee in the early 1850s and built the Hill's Chapel church.

--Although Joab Short was unable to read or write, and was addicted to strong drink, he accumulated considerable property and slaves.

--From the estate of John Cash, dec'd, J. F. L. Fares, adm'r, November 2, 1863, reports: "The following Negroes came into my hands: Esther a woman age 28 years, Nelson a boy aged 10 years, Henry a boy 8 years, 1 boy Davis 4 years, 1 girl May 3 years, Ellen a girl 1 year, being in number 6." He goes on to tell about the slaves taken by the Union Army.

Basil B. McMahan in 1936 in his book, "Coffee County, Then and Now" tells of the following colored men and women who had resided in Coffee County:

--"'Uncle' Lindsley Brewer, ex-slave, brought to Manchester by Dr. J. E. Rodes in 1850, later owned by Captain C. C. Brewer. He was the first vendor of ice cream in Manchester. Originator of the famous "Fourth of August" colored celebration in Manchester, which is still an annual event among the darkies."

--"James (Big Jim) Wilson, faithful employee of a number of people in Manchester. Born in slavery."

-- "'Uncle' Luke Layne, whom upon being asked as a witness in court as to how long he had resided in Manchester, replied: "I have been here always.""

--"'Aunt' Mariah Peay, a darky of ante-bellum days, who lived to a ripe old age."

--"'Aunt' Mandy Wilson, wife of James Wilson, nurse for the white people."

--"Lucinda Wilson, ex-slave, mother of 10 children, including James Wilson, and for whom the "Lucy Hole" on Duck River was named, this being her place for washing clothes for white folks."

--"'Uncle' Alf Elliott, brick mason and builder, and famous weather prophet."

--"Robert Vannoy, contractor and builder, constructed many residences and business buildings in Manchester. Died several years ago."

--"'Aunt' Matilda Vannoy, famous cook and faithful church worker."

--"Jeff Elliott, famous fiddler and hunter."

--"Willis Baugh, employed by the N. C. & St. L. RR for more than 50 years."

In nothing was slavery so savage and relentless as in its attempted destruction of the family instincts of the Negro race in America. Individuals, not families; shelters, not homes; herding, not marriages, were the cardinal sins in that system of horrors.
~~Fannie Barrier Williams, "Black Women in Nineteenth-Century American Life"

1850 and 1860 MORTALITY SCHEDULES
OF COFFEE COUNTY

Most, but not all, slaves took on their owners' surnames, often changing surnames with each sale. Some chose to keep the name of a previous owner or adopted that of a person who had been kind to them. A good source in finding the given names of slaves is in mortality schedules. Although the surnames of the slaves are not given, they are listed after a white person, which may or may not have had the same sir name. They are given here with the preceding surnames. Listed below are the statistics from Schedules 3 of the Federal Censuses for 1850 and 1860, showing the persons who died during the year ending June 30. The time given at the end of each is the length of time the person had been sick. One hundred and thirty deaths occurred in Coffee County in 1850, 37 of them were slaves.

1850:

Angelina Barton, 4 year old, female slave born in NC, died in May suddenly from Fits.

Jenny Smith, 60 year old, female slave born in NC, died in Aug. of unknown causes - about 100 days.

Robert Anthony, 10 month old, male slave born in TN, died in Sept. from teething - 6 wks.

Cilla Roach, 7 month old, female slave born in TN, died in April of unknown causes - 6 wks.

William Roach, 3 month old, male slave born in TN, died in Feb. suddenly of unknown cause.

Bob Roach, 70 year old, male slave born in TN, died in Dec. of old age - 1 yr.

Candes Roach, 38 year old, female slave born in TN, died in Aug. of Scrofula - about 100 days.

Caroline Roach, 20 year old, female slave born in TN, died in Aug. of Scrofula – 5 yrs.

Lucinda Roach, 16 year old, female slave born in TN, died in Aug. of Scrofula – 6 yrs.

Bob Roach, 6 year old, male slave born in TN, died in Nov. of Measles – 7 days.

Ned Roach, 63 year old, male slave born in SC, died in Nov. of Consumption – about 100 days.

Eliza Duncan, 34 year old, female slave born in VA, died in April of unknown causes – 6 days.

Henry Wilson, 3 year old, male slave born in TN, died in July after 40 days of typhoid fever.

Mariah Wilson, 40 year old, female slave born in TN, died in Oct. after 8 days of Consumption.

Child Wilson, 1 month old, female slave born in TN, died in Mar. suddenly of unknown causes.

Child Wilson, 11 month old, male slave born in TN, died in July suddenly of unknown causes.

George Raburn, 2 month old, male slave born in TN, died in Dec. suddenly from smothering.

Edmond Niccols, 55 year old, male slave born in VA, died in July of unknown causes – 2 mos.

Esther Niccols, 7 year old, female slave born in TN, died in Aug. after 1 month of typhoid fever.

Tom Emerson, 50 year old, male slave born in VA, died in Jan. of Dropsy – 3 mos.

Tom Taylor, 8 month old, male slave born in TN, died in July suddenly from an accident.

Elizabeth Taylor, 5 month old, female slave born in TN, died in Jan. of Inflammation of brain – 8 days.

Molly Baker, 85 year old, female slave born in SC, died in July of old age – 2 wks.

Reuben Baker, 25 year old, male slave born in TN, died in Feb. of Fits – 3 wks.

Alfred Baker, 50 year old, male slave, birth place unknown, died in May after 6 months of a spinal affliction.

Priscilla Baker, 35 year old, female slave born in TN, died in Sept. of a cold – 7 days.

Infant Baker, 8 month old, female slave born in TN, died in July suddenly of unknown causes.

Isaac Price, 42 year old, male slave born in VA, died in Sept. of typhoid fever – 3 wks.

Winny Price, 28 year old, female slave born in SC, died in Aug. of typhoid fever – 2 wks.

Mary Price, 11 year old, female slave born in TN, died in Aug of typhoid fever – 2 wks.

Peter Price, 8 year old, male slave born in TN, died in Sept. of typhoid fever – 2 wks.

Joseph Price, 6 month old, male slave born in TN, died in Sept. of typhoid fever – 7 days.

John Thompson, 2 year old, male slave born in TN, died in Nov. from poisoning – 3 days.

Jane Inmon, 21 year old, female slave born in TN, died in June of typhoid fever – 8 days.

Judy Inmon, 3 month old, female, mulatto slave born in TN, died in June from Diarrhea – 2 wks.

Haney Payne, 60 year old, female slave, birthplace unknown, died in Mar of unknown causes – 2 days.

Mariah Sparkman, 25 year old, female slave, birthplace unknown, died in Jan of typhoid fever – 2 months.

1860:

Bob Keele, 24 year old, male slave born in TN, died in Aug. of a lingering Pock.

Miranda Keele, 33 year old, female slave born in TN, died in May of Dropsy after 90 days of illness. Miranda was listed as a Servant.

Cleo Pinson, 100 year old, female slave, died in July of old age.

Gun Pinson, 1 year old, male slave born in TN, died in December of the Croup.

Margaret Pinson, 38 year old, female slave born in TN, died in May of a lingering cancer. Margaret was listed as a Cook.

Mary Claybrook, 74 year old, female slave born in TN, a Domestic Servant died in Feb. No cause given.

Caroline Claybrook, 4 year old, female slave born in TN, died in Aug. of Scrofula – 20 days.

Harriett Hill, 2 year old, female slave born in TN, died in May of Whooping Cough – 14 days.

Matilda Ensey, 25 year old, female slave born in TN, a Cook, died in May from child birth – 6 days.

Clairy Norton, 16 year old, female slave born in TN, died in Sept. from child birth – 7 days.

Lydia Penson, 70 year old, female slave born in TN, died in June of old age.

Charles Johnson, 82 year old, male slave born in TN, died in Nov. of old age.

Priss Johnson, 22 year old, female slave born in TN, died in June of unknown causes.

Frances Henry, 10 year old, female slave born in TN, died in Sept. of typhoid fever – 13 days.

Ben McMahan, 9 month old, male slave born in TN, died in May of unknown causes – 14 days.

Sandy McMahan, 11 month old, female slave born in TN, died in March of the Croup – 1 day.

[Typhoid: serious disease spread by contaminated food and water. **Consumption: pulmonary TB **Dropsy**: swelling of soft tissues due to the accumulation of excess water. **Lingering pock** (Pick's disease?): Dementia. **Croup**: a type of respiratory infection. **Scofula**: an infection in the lymph nodes]

"Whenever I hear anyone arguing for slavery, I feel a strong impulse to see it tried on him personally."
~~Abraham Lincoln, speech, March 17, 1865

"Manchester has the best lot of Negroes in the state"
~~Manchester Times, March 8, 1905

SLAVE PROPERTY DISPOSED OF IN LAST WILLS AND TESTAMENTS

There are sources where the names of slaveholders can be learned, but it is seldom that the actual names of slaves are given. The last wills and testaments of the slaveholders is another good source to learn given names. Slaves, being property, were disposed of in the same manner in which one might dispense of household goods, livestock, or real estate. The following are excerpts from Coffee County wills where slaves are mentioned:

From the will of JACOB KEELE, dated Nov. 26, 1852: "...I direct that at the death of my said wife all my property except the slaves be sold... ...I bequeath to my beloved daughter Mary Sparks and the heirs of her body, my negro girl Eliza, said slave to be valued. Also, I give to my beloved daughter Sarah and the heirs of her body, my negro girl Nancy, said slave to be also valued. I further direct that the balance of my slaves be valued by disinterested man and divided by lot among all my other children except Mary Sparks and Sarah, so that in the division of my slave property each child shall receive an equal share. It is my will that the said slaves Eliza and Nancy or either of them should die before the division of my other slaves and property, that my daughters Mary and Sarah shall have equal shares with the other children of said slaves."

WILLIAM DANIEL SR., Feb. 27, 1836: "...to my beloved wife Elizabeth Daniel ... also these slaves (to wit) Charles, Dinah and her natural increase and Sarah during her natural life or widowhood and at her death the above named property is to be equally divided among her eight children to wit ... I then direct that my land on Riley's Creek and my negro man John to be sold and the money which they bring be divided ..."

SANDFORD BERRY, Aug. 25, 1836: "... I will that my son William Berry have an equal share with my legatees with the exception of two hundred dollars which he received and a negro man Minga. ... I will that my daughter Namin Frazier have an equal share with my legatees with the exception of three hundred dollars for which she received and a negro woman. ... I will that my daughter Elizabeth Jones have no divide with my legatees she having received to the amount of eight hundred dollars in Negro property given also by deed of Gift ..."

THOMAS KING, June 8, 1836: "...to my daughter Hannah Parten a negro girl Ann about eight months old which she has in her possession for her own separate use and benefit and not for the use, benefit or control of her said husband during my said daughter's natural life and at her death the said negro girl and her increase to be divided among the children of my said daughter Hannah Parten."

THOMAS HARRISON, Sept. 11, 1838: "...I loan to my beloved wife Nancy Harrison the plantation on which I now live and of my negroes and their further increase to wit: Nannie and Diley and Carroline and James and Isaac and Mary and all my horses... then at her death all of my estate to be equally divided among my seven children, to wit: ..."

DAVID CONLSON, Feb. 21, 1833: "...and over and above the equal share given to my beloved wife (Sarah Conlson) it is my will and wish that she shall have choice of a Negro man and woman in addition for and during her natural life, and at her death the whole and every part of her share of my estate ... to be equally distributed and divided between the whole of my children."

JAMES OAKS, Jan. 7, 1841: "...I desire for the black woman Lucretia to be hired out after the expiration of the present year and the yellow boy Jim as soon as he is large enough both to be hired out yearly until the land is sold or divided among my heirs and I want my beloved wife to keep the other little girl named Rose until the division of the land to help raise the children and then all the Negroes and their increase and the proceeds of the hire and the proceeds arising from the sale or rent of the Harp place if there should be any and equally divided among my heirs

CHARLES L. ROACH, Oct. 2, 1844: "...to (my) mother Elizabeth Roach and Phebe Brown (my) sister her lifetime and at his mother's death a certain negro slave girl by the name of Martha. I give the slave girl Martha to my sister Phebe Brown and to her bodily heirs forever, the said girl to wait as much on one of them as the other until my mother's death."

WILLIAM SHED, Sept. 8, 1840: "...Also one boy..."

21

JOSEPH CARNEY, Feb. 22, 1841: "... unto my beloved wife Mary during her lifetime the following Negroes viz. Hector, Monday, Indy, Judy, Patzy and child of Pegys during her natural life. ...I give to my daughter Noahmah my Negro Woman Patty and her child and negro girl Edy and boys Tony and Davy. ...The negro woman Patey (sic) and her child however to remain as first stated with my beloved wife during her lifetime. ...I also bequeath unto my grandson Legrand H. Carney the following Negroes viz: Monday and George, the Negro Monday however as first to remain with my wife Mary during her natural life and then to be my grandson Legrand H Carney's. I also wish that my Negro man Tom be sold and four hundred dollar of his price be given to Isabelle Taylor if she lives to be ten years old and when she arrives at that age, and the balance of the price of Tom I will and bequeath to my grandson Legrand H Carney. I, however, make this provision, that if Legrand H. Carney prefer keeping Tom and paying the four hundred dollars that he shall do so. It is my wish and will that Tom shall have a selection of his master if sold. I will and bequeath unto my grandson Sanders B. Carney my Negro man Peter and all my black-smith tools... ...my grandson L. A. Carney should see proper to farm on that portion of land above mentioned, that my Negro woman Cherry and Nannie shall remain thereon, not subjects not as slaves to him but their labor to be for their benefit, but in case he should keep any hands here it is my wish that Cherry shall be placed under the care and charge of Grandson Smith Carney and that Nannie be placed under care and charge of my Grandson Sanders R. Carney, neither of them do I wish to be considered servants or slaves in any wise, but that they be permitted to use their own labor for their own support. I bequeath unto my granddaughter Susan Sparks my Negro woman Clarissa provided she is willing to go to her, but if not it is my wish that she shall be sold in the neighborhood of her husband belonging to Wilson Norton and that the preference be given to said Norton to purchase her upon said terms for cash or part cash and the balance on time and the proceeds to be given to my granddaughter Susan, above mentioned..." CODICIL, March 14, 1841: "It is my will and desire that my Grandson P. Harrison should have at my death my Negro boy Josh..."

DUNCAN NEIL, May 30, 1840: "...and all of my movable property to be sold and the proceeds to be divided among the following heirs excepting my servant John who shall not be sold under six years after my death but shall remain as a slave on the plantation for the benefit of the family who resides here and then to be sold and to be disposed of as the balance of the property..."

HUGH DAVIDSON, Sept. 14, 1841: "...to my beloved wife Jane the following perishable property to wit: My negro man Ben, my negro man Lambert, my negro woman Hannah, my negro girl Ann, my negro girl Mary, also my negro man Andy, also all my stock ... to my daughter Pricilla Britton one Negro girl named Ibby worth three hundred dollars which she has already gotten... ...to my daughter Margaret Guinn one negro girl worth four hundred... ...to my son David W. Davidson one negro boy named Gradison worth three hundred dollars which he has got... ...to my daughter Angelina Morgan one Negro girl Mary worth three hundred and fifty dollars which she has got and had in her possession and disposed of... ...to my son John Davidson one negro man named Kit worth seven hundred dollars which he has already got... ...to my son Samuel L. Davidson one negro man Isaac worth seven hundred dollars which he has got ... ...to my son Hugh Davidson one negro boy Alfred worth five hundred dollars... ...to my son Robert B. Davidson my negro boy Henderson worth three hundred dollars ... ...to my daughter Marthy Ann Davidson my Negro girl Caroline worth five hundred dollars..."

MORTON JONES, May 30, 1840: I give and bequeath to Nancy Jane my dearly beloved wife all my property to wit: my negro boy Sammy..."

WILLIAM BOWDEN, May 21, 1842: "...unto my beloved wife Nancy ... the plantation ... for her to do with as she pleases and after her death the plantation where I now live is to belong to my two youngest sons viz. Fredrick McBowden and G. L. Bowden, ... (to Frederick McBowden)... the Negroes Daniel and Priscella and my son G. L. Bowden I leave two Negroes named Louiza and Ben extra of their share after the death of my wife..."

ELIZABETH DOUGLASS, Feb. 9, 1839: "...to my son Benjamin Douglass ... all my personal property consisting of a negro woman Jane and a girl Catherine ..."

JOSEPH WILLIS, May 1, 1843: "I will and bequeath to my beloved wife Bitzy Ann Willis all the land belonging to me with all my negroes, horses, cattle, hogs, sheep..."

JACOB HOOVER, May 24, 1843: "...to my son Mathias Hoover one negro boy about 5 years old named Caleb ...my son Julius Hoover one negro girl about 18 years old named Dinah and her increase ...my son Simeon Hoover one negro man named Jacob about 22 years old ...my son Martin Hoover one negro man about 25 years old named Frank ...my daughter Elizabeth Rowling one negro man named Joe about 40 years old ...my wife Polly Hoover one negro boy about 2 years old named John ...my son Henry Hoover one negro woman named Clary about 50 years old..."

ROBERT S. RAYBURN, Dec. 31, 1844: "...It is my desire that should my beloved wife die during widowhood ... that my land and slaves be either divided or sold as my executors may think best... It is my desire that my slave Cleo remain in the family and should she at any time become a charge I want her maintained of the estate."

ELIZABETH WALLACE, April 9, 1845: "...to my daughter Nancy three negroes Lucy, Alexander and Mary ...to my daughter Elizabeth Lambert and her heirs three negroes Jacob, Marthae and Jim."

DUNCAN NEIL, Nov. 28, 1840: "...all my moveable property to be sold and the proceeds divided among the following heirs excepting my servant John who shall not be sold under six years after my decease but shall remain as a slave on the plantation for the benefit of the family who resides there and then to be sold and to be disposed of as the balance of the property."

JOHN HICKERSON, July 16, 1845: "...all my negroes and other property go with my wife during her lifetime subject to her control and that the labor of my negroes over and above that may be necessary to the support of my wife go to the payment of what debts I may owe ...(and if) not sufficient to pay my debts ... my executors are directed to sell such of the negroes or other property as may be necessary..."

JAMES CUNNINGHAM, Aug. 27, 1845: "...my wife then Polly or Mary Hollingsworth ... should have the power to dispose of her land and the following negroes by will to wit: Alfred, Anthony, Matilda and Micy and their increase, at present three in number to wit: Sam and Preston sons of Matilda and George son of Micy. ...I also give and bequeath to my said son Rowley Cunningham one negro man now in his possession named Samsone... ...upon the marriage of my said daughter (Sinai Harris) I gave her a negro girl named Emily who has been lately sold to satisfy the debts of her husband at which sale I became the purchaser and have again given her to my said daughter ... in any division of my estate neither her nor her heirs are to be charged with said girl (now a woman) upon the first or second gift. The balance of my estate ... to my children and grandchildren ... provided that in the division of the slaves I expressly enjoin it upon my executor as well as my children not to separate the men and their wives without their consent... To my daughter Elizabeth Crocker I have advanced a negro girl Arminda at the price of one hundred and seventy five dollars..."

EDMOND KEELING, Jan. 8, 1846: "I will and bequeath my negro boy John to my two sons John and Elsy, but that he shall remain with the family for their support until the youngest child becomes of age... It is then my wish that my two sons shall dispose of him as they think proper."

THOMAS BLAIR, Dec. 24, 1845: "...to my beloved wife Eleanor my negro man Cy about 40 years of age... ...the balance of my lands, negroes and other property be sold and proceeds thereof be equally divided..."

ABNER DUNCAN, Jan. 3, 1847: "...I also leave to her (Anne Duncan) ... Vincy and her youngest children, that is Martin, Cloe and Rosanna with the privilege of keeping Tom as long as she can manage him...for the purpose of helping raise her children but whenever he becomes unmanageable it is my desire she hand him over to my executor to hire out. The balance of my negroes with the exception of Creasy and her child, viz. that is David, Dick and Jack I desire my executor may hire out being particular to have them well treated. Having had in contemplation for some time to sell Creasy and her child ...my executor sell them for the best price he can get at private sale, for that purpose Rolley Cunningham is wanting to purchase and she being desirous to go then it is my wish he may get her if he will give as good a price as any one else."

SARAH NICHOLS, Dec. 13, 1843: "...I also give Cynthia Nichols a promissory note ... for $2919.00 for a family of negroes sold by me to Cynthia..."

JOHNATHAN PHILLIPS, March 1, 1847: "I give to my wife Sarah Phillips ... one mulatto man named Lewis..."

F. W. BOWDEN, June 20, 1848: "...That I wish the two negroes Daniel and Prisella to fall back to father's estate and be divided as father's will directs..."

ADAM RAYBURN, Aug, 13, 1849: "...I desire that all my property remain in the possession of my beloved wife Sarah Rayburn until my children become of age or marry at which time if they desire they can each have a negro ... reserving to my aforesaid wife my negro woman Caroline and in case she should die any one of the other women that she may choose..."

WILLIAM S. WATTERSON, July 2, 1851: "...my beloved wife Nancy Watterson ...she is also to select three negro men to cultivate her farm and two negro women and boy and one girl. ...my son Thomas H... I also give him my negro boy George to make him equal with the other children who have already received a negro apiece. ...I nominate ... Andrew Maxwell and William B. Watterson my executors ... to devise or sell the slaves on hand not otherwise disposed of..."

DAVID HICKERSON, Oct. 10, 1851: "My boy Jim I desire to be hired out at Shelbyville for the year 1852 at the end of that time I desire him to be sold. ...the aforesaid land and negroes to be sold by my executors hereinafter named upon a credit..."

CHARLES MOORE, Dec. 31, 1850: "...to my beloved wife Mary Moore ... five negroes, to wit: Charles, Mariah, Manuel, Matty and her child Ann and their future increase... ...to my daughter Sarah F. Shanklin during her natural life and then to her children a Negro girl named Rachael and her future increase, said Negro to be valued to her by disinterested men ... and which is not to be subject to the payment of her husband's debts, and should a share amount to more than the value of said Negro, the amount above that to be placed in the hands of trustee and for her to draw annually the interest thereon to use... ...the balance of my Negroes not named above be valued by disinterested men and put into lots and drawn for and divided as follows to wit: that

William Moore and Benjamin Moore, Shophia Finch, Jane Scrugs, Susan Hoover and Eliza Thomas each draw a share to make them equal to Sarah F. Shanklin and that the two children of my son Robert Moore, deceased, draw only a half share between them and that Martha A. Moore, daughter of Martha Moore deceased draw a half share... ...At the death of my wife I will that the Negroes she may have be valued and divided as above specified..."

REUBEN CARDEN, April 21, 1852: I will my wife... to have Peter and Clark and Matilda, three Negroes, two boys and one girl, and the tract of land that I live on ... and at her death my son Robert C. Carden is to have a Negro boy named Peter and a girl named Martha which I bought of the two Nortons, and Harris and all the property his mother has except Clark and Matilda, two Negroes. William L. Carden to have a Negro boy named Jerry and Martin A. Carden to have a Negro boy called Clark and Lucinda J. Jackson (to have Matilda?)..."

CHARLOTTE S. THOMPSON, May 17, 1853: "...to my son Burwell J. Thompson, one Negro man named Henry, aged about thirty five, one Negro boy named John, six or seven years old, one Negro girl named Amanda, seven years old, and all other property that I may die seized and possessed of..."

JOHN WILSON, April 29, 1854: "...to my sister, Jane C. Wilson ... my Negro woman Mary and one of her children, namely, John Beel, during her lifetime ... to my niece, Francis Tate, one Negro girl named Phebe to her and the heirs of her body, also one bed and furniture..."

WILLIAM CUNNINGHAM, Nov. 2, 1853: "...to my wife during her life or widowhood all of lands and Negroes and all other property of every species that I may possess ..."

JESSE JENKINS, July 26, 1845: "...to my beloved wife Nancy Jenkins ... two negroes viz Peter and Phebe ... ...All the above property ... then to descend and go to my three sons viz William G., Benjamin F. and James N. Jenkins and the children of my said three sons, that is the legal legitimate heirs of their body... My negro woman Nelly who is advanced in life and one of the mother of the family and has been a faithful servant, I leave her under the protection of my said three sons but not to be considered in the capacity of a slave... ...I give and bequeath unto my beloved son William G.

Jenkins my Negro boy Sam, that is to say he is to have the use and labor of said boy during his natural life and then descend to and be possessed by the legal and legitimate heirs of his body... ...to my son Benjamin F. my Negro boy Henry... ...to my beloved son James N. my Negro boy George Senr., both the latter boys, that is Henry and George, to be under the Regulations and Restrictions that Samuel the farmer is under... ...The negroes to be equally divided among my said three sons as may be but none of them to be sold under any circumstances whatever except Jack if it should be advisable or become really necessary that it should be done from some source or other the proceeds to be applied as above directed if the said Jack has to be sold, my earnest wish is that he may be sold into as good hands as possible... ...If my said negro woman Nelly should become unable to labor she is to be supported from my said estate..." CODICIL, Dec. 10, 1847: "Since writing the within which was my last will and testament the Negro girl therein by me bequeathed to my beloved wife Nancy Jenkins has died which makes it necessary for the benefit of my said wife to so far alter the within will that instead of Peter and Phebe as bequeathed to her in the last will I bequeath and give to her a choice of any three Negroes that I may die possessed of to her and belong to her during her natural life and (thereafter) to go and be possessed as directed in said last will and testament..."

JAMES SHEID, Jan. 19, 1853: "...to my beloved wife Sibbil Sheed (sic)... the following Negroes to be my wife's during her natural life or widowhood: Becca, Millia, Suk and Sarah, and then to descend to and be equally divided among my four sons (viz) William R. Sheed, Jesse J. Sheed, James M. Shed (sic) and Henry S. Sheed..."

ELIAS TEAL, March 6, 1856: (The first part of this will is given earlier in this article in reference to freed blacks being sent to Liberia) "...I do nominate and appoint W. R. McFadin of the County of Rutherford guardian of my said children and desire him when they become old enough to start to school and sooner if necessary to take them and raise them and attend to their education..."

"...Also, should my executors think proper they may let my slave Martha attend them (the children) to wait on them... ...I also wish my slaves well fed and clothed and suitably attended in sickness ..." CODICIL, Sept. 10, 1856: "...I desire now that instead of keeping up the farm my executors shall hire out all the Negroes except the one to go with the children and rent out the farm annually ... ...It is also my express will that my executors shall not rent the farm or hire any of the Negroes to any of my relatives..."

MARY CARNEY, Nov. 24, 1856: Mary Carney ... in her last sickness living with Smith Carney, died on the above day, called her Grandson Smith unto her while she was lying in bed and told her Grandson Smith Carney to settle with Legsand who is her grandson also, the said Legsand Carney for the hire of a Negro man by the name of Monday ..."

HULDA MASON, Oct. 4, 1856: "...to my brother Asa Thomas my Negro woman Caroline and her four children, Cynna, Moss, Mary and Martha during his natural life... ...but he is to permit the girl Cynna to live with Mrs. Stephens, wife of Elmathen Stephens, so long as Mrs. Stephens resides in Middle Tennessee. Upon her death or removal from Middle Tennessee, said girl to be delivered to said Asa Thomas for life as above stated... ...My negro man Drew I desire to be set free, but as I cannot do that I will him to my brother, Asa Thomas, who I know will take care of him as he is now old and as he has been a faithful servant. I desire him well cared for and he may become a charge upon my said brother. I give him one hundred dollars to enable him to take care of him... ...My other negroes, Ben and Tena and Tena's child as well as all money on hand ... to be equally divided among my brothers, share and share alike, except Asa Thomas who is not to have any portion further than as above provided for him... ...The stock etc. will have to be sold in order to divide the proceeds but the Negroes I do not want sold if they can justly be divided..."

CHARLES TIMMONS, Feb. 14, 1859: "...my negroes and perishable property be sold and the proceeds equally divided between ... Ambrose, Priscella Hodge, Thomas, Virginia M. Lindey, Mattory (Matery, Matory) Tuck, Malinda, and Susan provided that Malinda and Susan have received their four hundred dollars each, Mattory her two hundred dollars before an equal division is made..."

AMBROSE TIMMONS, Sept. 29, 1856: "...at the death of my said wife, I direct that all the property be equally divided between all my children, except my unfortunate little daughter Effie who is blind. She is to have a choice Negro to be selected by her at her mother's death over and above an equal share with the other children..."

1850 SLAVERY and FREE BLACKS STATISTICS

The population of Coffee County had been increasing gradually. In 1840 there were 7,057 white inhabitants, 1,085 slaves, and 22 free Negroes for a total of 8,164. In 1850 the census showed a small increase: there were 7,061 white inhabitants, 1,264 slaves and 12 free Negroes for a total of 8,337. Although 239 people owned slaves, the majority owned fewer than ten. Arthur M. Rutledge was one of the exceptions, and the largest slaveholder in the county with 50 slaves. Although he owned land and slaves in the county, he may not have actually lived here. He may have resided in Davidson County at that time, leaving an overseer to manage his plantation. In 1860 he is found on the Franklin County census.

The summary given at the end of the 1850 census shows there were 23 free blacks in Coffee County at the time, but numerous combings of the records turn up only 13. Listed here with age, sex, color and occupation are those thirteen:

Free Blacks in 1850:

NAME	AGE	SEX	COLOR	OCCUPATION
Angel, Mary	65	F	Mulatto	None given
Baine, Andrew	25	M	Mulatto	Laborer
Clark, Jinny	67	F	Black	None given
Crawford, Joseph	6	M	Mulatto	None
Haggerty, Judy	95	F	Black	None given
Haggerty, Peter	100	M	Black	Laborer
Halpin, Jaw	2	F	Mulatto	None
Hagis, Claig	50	F	Mulatto	None given
Ishom, Jack	22	M	Mulatto	Blacksmith
Simpson, David	22	M	Black	Laborer
Smith, Elizabeth J.	27	F	Mulatto	None given

| Thompson, Judith | 65 | F | Black | None given |
| Vituch (?), Henry | 22 | M | Black | None given |

Of the 239 slaveholders in 1850, 172 were farmers. Other occupations break down as follows: 9 clergymen, 8 merchants, 2 saddlers, 3 blacksmiths, 1 bookseller, 2 manufacturers, 5 physicians, 1 attorney, 1 stage contractor, 1 miller, 2 laborer, 2 inn keepers, 1 wheel right, 1 wagon wright, 1 tanner, 1 school teacher, 1 RR contractor, and 25 that were not given, or are unknown.

Below is the list of slave owners from the 1850 census, including their age, occupation and the number of slaves owned:

1850 Slave Owners:

Allison, Thomas	50	Farmer	1
Allison, Thomas		Farmer	1
Arnold, John	70	Farmer	2
Ashley, James	53	Farmer	7
Ashley, William	60	Farmer	7
Austille, Amos	75	Farmer	17
Austille, Samuel	39	Farmer	6
Austille, William	35	Farmer	4
Baily, John R.	51	Farmer	2
Barton, Abner	48	Farmer	6
Barton, Benjamin	28	Farmer	1
Bashaw, Joseph	39	Inn Keeper	4
Bird, Samuel	26	Farmer	1
Blair, R. D.	32	Merchant	2
Blanton, Newton	24	Farmer	5

Blanton, Smith	32	Farmer	7
Blanton, Willis	40	Farmer	10
Bowdon, G. E.	30	Farmer	9
Boyd, F. M.	28	Farmer	1
Brantley, James A.	42	Saddler	1
Brixey, Walton	44	Farmer	1
Brown, Rudman	32	Farmer	2
Bryan, Abner	46	Farmer	3
Bryan, John	38	Farmer	9
Bryan, Matthew	44	Farmer	6
Buckaloo, James	29	Farmer	1
Buckaloo, William A.	25	Farmer	1
Butler, Moses	27	Farmer	1
Call, Daniel H.	59	Farmer	3
Campbell, Mary M	55	None given	8
Carden, Reuben	45	Farmer	5
Cargile, Thomas	23	Farmer	7
Carlile, James	38	Farmer	2
Carney, Smith	45	Farmer	10
Cash, James	26	Farmer	1
Cash, John	55	Farmer	8
Caulson, Charles	52	Farmer	4
Chapman, George W.	40	Blacksmith	6
Charles, John	56	Wagon Rgt	4
Clark, James	27	Farmer	3
Cole, Isaac	50	Farmer	4
Conn, William	53	Meth Clerg	1
Cook, Oliver	33	Blacksmith	1
Crawford, Joseph	50	CP Clerg	3
Crockett, John	70	Farmer	14

Crockett, Samuel J.	41	Farmer	7
Cunningham, John	42	Farmer	20
Cunningham, Nancy	35	None	2
Cunningham, Nancy	27	Farmer wife	4
Cunningham, Rawleigh	53	WheelRgt	1
Cunningham, William	40	Farmer	5
Cunningham, William	40	Miller	5
Daniel, Elizabeth	71	None list	3
Darnell, James	33	Merchant	1
Davidson, David	46	Farmer	3
Davidson, Hugh	55	Farmer	10
Davidson, Jane	72	None (farmers in household)	14
Davidson, Samuel L.	38	Farmer	11
Davis, A. B.	38	Physician	8
Dean, John	70	Farmer	2
Downing, Alexander	49	Farmer	5
Drake, Catherine	64	None given	2
Duggan, B. F.	30	Meth Clerg	1
Duncan, Ann	31	None	5
Elliott, Stephen	62	Farmer	6
Ewell, Dabney	60	Physician	9
Farrar, John	76	Farmer	6
Farrar, William	52	Farmer	4
Farris, John	39	Farmer	8
Finch, Sophia	43	None list	8
Foster, Hugh	56	Farmer	1
Foster, Hugh A.	28	Tanner	2
Gather, Rebecca	50	None given	2
Gibson, William B.	37	Farmer	7
Gotcher, Jesse	54	Farmer	1

Green, James	50	None given – Son a farmer	2
Gunn, Michael	43	Farmer	1
Gunn, Thomas L.	39	Farmer	5
Haggard, Robert M.	30	Meth Clerg	4
Hagins, Clara	50	None	1
Ham, Norman J.	46	Farmer	7
Hampton, Ransom	45	Farmer	2
Hancock, Martin	51	Farmer	5
Hardaway, Benjamin F.	33	Meth Clerg	1
Harpe, Celia	57	None	1
Harris, Lewis	45	Farmer	1
Heiss, Joseph D.	58	Farmer	3
Herriford, John	43	Stage Cont	2
Hickerson, Charles	38	Farmer	8
Hickerson, Charles	31	Farmer	5
Hickerson, David	28	Farmer	5
Hickerson, David	63	Farmer	1
Hickerson, Joseph	24	Book Seller	1
Hickerson, Joseph	61	Farmer	22
Hickerson, Little	25	Farmer	3
Hickerson, Nancy	68	None – son farmer	24
Hickerson, William	33	Attorney-at-law	14
Hickerson, William A.	36	Merchant	1
Hindman, John	32	School teacher	1
Hodge, John	65	Farmer	2
Hodge, William	66	Farmer	19
Holland, Benjamin	66	Merchant	2
Holland, Ed	35	Farmer	3
Holland, Sarah	60	None given	1
Hoover, Martin	32	Farmer	1

Hord, C. F.	36	RR Contractor	25
Hord, Colman			3
Hough, James E.	28	Physician	2
Howard, John P.	54	Farmer	4
Howard, Sarah	76	None	2
Howe, Joseph	36	Farmer	3
Hufman, John	49	Farmer	2
Jacobs, Alfred	31	Farmer	3
Jacobs, Jeremiah	59	Farmer	20
Jarnigan, G. W.	27	Merchant	1
Jenkins, Benjamin	40	Farmer	8
Jenkins, Jesse	77	Farmer	15
Johnson, James	26	Farmer	2
Johnson, John	47	Farmer	6
Keele, Jacob	60	Farmer	11
Keele, William	32	Farmer	9
Keeling, James	41	Farmer	3
Keeling, Mary	73	None given	5
Keller, S. C.	26	Manufacturer (Hough)	2
Lambert, Robert	28	Farmer	1
Lasater, Robert E.	33	Keeper of Hotel	3
Lavender, William	42	Farmer	1
Layne, Benjamin	43	Farmer	13
Layne, Wyatt	47	Farmer	11
Ledbetter, Mary	68	None	1
Lusk, Isaac	61	Farmer	3
Lusk, Joseph	46	Farmer	1
Martin, Langston	39	Farmer	1
Martin, Margaret	48	None given	1
Mason, James	61	Farmer	10

Mason, Thomas	43	Farmer	4
Maxwell, Andrew	42	Farmer	13
McBee, (Magby), Silas	56	Farmer	6
McDaniel, William K.	41	Manufacturer (Hough)	1
McMichael, Alexander	52	Farmer	2
McMichael, William	49	Farmer	4
Meadows, Littleton	32	Farmer	1
Miller, George	50	Farmer	16
Montgomery, Susan	35	None given	2
Moore, Benjamin	25	Merchant	3
Moore, Charles	74	Farmer	12
Morrow Samuel	30	Farmer	1
Neville, Lucy	39	None given	8
Neville, Pleasant	44	Farmer	2
Nichols, Cynthia	51	None given	4
Norton, Henry W.	33	Farmer	2
Norton, Henry Wilson	84	Methodist Clergyman	4
Norton, N. P.	30	Farmer	6
Norton, Norman	73	Farmer	3
Norton, Norman G.	40	Farmer	4
Norton, William S.	63	Farmer	8
Patton, John	57	Farmer	7
Patton, Joseph	32	Merchant	2
Philips, James	46	Farmer	3
Phillips, Lorenzo	42	Methodist Clergyman	2
Phillips, Micajah	28	Farmer	1
Phillips, Sarah	45	None given	1
Phillips, William	28	Farmer	1
Phillips, William	50	Farmer	2
Pirtle, Robert	29	Farmer	1

Poindexter, Amanda	35	None – Son farmer	1
Powell, Alexander	64	Farmer	8
Powers, Henry	50	Farmer	5
Powers, John H.	25	Farmer	2
Powers, Thomas	58	Farmer	17
Price, Pleasant H.	37	Farmer	12
Price, Reuben	49	Farmer	1
Price, Richard	51	Farmer	5
Pully, Gideon	62	Farmer	11
Raburn, Mary	50	None – son farmer	5
Rankin, John	25	Farmer	2
Rayburn, Sarah	49	None- Son farmer	14
Reagan, Robert	55	Farmer	7
Reynolds, Hosea	58	Farmer	5
Reynolds, Mrs.	53	None given	1
Rhodes Thomas	45	Farmer	9
Richards, William	39	Farmer	1
Richardson, James	80	Farmer	1
Richardson, Thomas E.	30	Farmer	1
Roach, George	30	Farmer	3
Rogers, William	30	Farmer	2
Rowland, Charles	73	Farmer	1
Rowland, Jacob	54	Farmer	6
Rowlings, Sarah	2	None given	1
Rutledge, Arthur M.		Farmer	50
Samuel Hancock	43	Farmer	15
Sheid, James Jr.	36	Farmer	4
Sheid, James Sr.	71	Farmer	13
Sherrill, Uriah	47	Baptist Clergyman	9
Shipp, Ewel	63	Farmer	5

Skean, Davidson	28	Blacksmith	1
Smith, William	54	Laborer	1
Sparkman, Hardy	47	Farmer	7
Stephens, James M.	40	Farmer	12
Stephens, Thomas	45	Farmer	7
Stephenson, Thomas P.	42	Physician	1
Stephenson, William	70	Farmer	8
Stone, Nobel L.	56	Farmer	1
Stroud, B. F.	26	Farmer	2
Stroud, Walter	44	Farmer	6
Tally, Jacob C.	24	Farmer	8
Taylor, Elizabeth	57	None	1
Taylor, James	44	Farmer	8
Taylor, Robert	46	Farmer	2
Teal, Elias	52	Farmer	11
Thompson, Charlotte	55	None given	8
Thompson, John	49	Farmer	7
Timmins, Ambrose	40	Farmer	1
Toliver, Jesse	60	Farmer	1
Turner, Elijah	37	Farmer	4
Wagoner, Ransome	39	Farmer	1
Waite, George	60	Farmer	6
Walker, John	53	Farmer	10
Watterson, William B.	29	CP Clergyman	5
Watterson, William S.	62	Farmer	23
Webster, Jonathan L.	29	Farmer	2
Wileman, John	81	Farmer	5
Wileman, Lawson	37	Merchant	1
Wileman, Manly	48	Farmer	7
Wileman, William	33	Farmer	2

Wilkinson, Isaac M.	38	Farmer	7
Wilkinson, Wm. C.	34	Farmer	2
Williams, W. B.	38	Saddler	1
Williams, William M.	36	Physician	2
Willis, Elizabeth	52	None given	17
Willis, John G.	30	Farmer	1
Wilson, Benny	30	Farmer	1
Wilson, John	49	Farmer	3
Wilson, John	50	Farmer	5
Wilson, Nancy	77	None given	1
Wilson, Robert	40	Farmer	2
Winton, John	50	Farmer	9
Winton, Stephen	57	Farmer	25
Wooten, William	33	Farmer	1

1860 SLAVERY and FREE BLACKS STATISTICS

1860 saw a decrease of free blacks in the county. The 8 listed below, along with their age, sex, color and occupations are:

Angel, Mary	60	F	Mulatto	Domestic Servant
Elliott, Elizabeth	38	F	Mulatto	Domestic Servant
Elliott, John H.	22	M	Mulatto	Farm Hand
Elliott, James	20	M	Mulatto	Farm Hand
Elliott, Elizabeth	14	F	Mulatto	
Elliott, Richard	10	M	Mulatto	
Elliott, Jackson	7	M	Mulatto	
Hancock, Mary	15	F	Mulatto	Domestic Servant

By 1860 the total population of the County was 9,689 inhabitants; 306 were the owners of 1,546 slaves. At this time, a farmer named Thomas Powers was the largest slaveholder, owning 36 slaves and 3 slave houses. The majority of the slaveholders had between 1 and 3 slaves.   Again, farming was the major industry (208), and the other slave owner occupations break down as follows: 6 farmer and merchants, 1 farmer and minister, 1 doctor and farmer, 9 clergymen, 9 merchants, 8 carpenters, 6 physicians, 4 blacksmiths, 2 sawyers, 2 inn keepers, 1 bookseller, 1 brick maker, 1 brick mason, 1 circuit clerk, 1 manufacturers, 1 attorney, 1 druggist, 1 liveryman, 1 com. laborer, 1 store clerk, 1 sheriff, 1 shoemaker, 1 surveyor, 1 teacher, 16 listed as domestic, and 19 with occupations that were not given, or are unknown.

Below is the list of slave owners from the 1860 census, including their age, occupation and the number of slaves owned:

1860 Slave Owners:

Name	Age	Occupation	No. Slaves
Anderson, O. P.	83	None	13
Arnold, John	40	Farmer	3
Arnold, Wm.	43	Farmer	2
Ashley, Wm.	71	Farmer	7
Ashly, Arthur	32	Farmer	8
Ashly, John	36	Farmer	1
Ashly, Lucy	54	Domestic	11
Ashly, Wm.	26	Farmer	2
Austill, L. B.	44	Farmer	16
Austille, S.	50	Farmer	10
Austille, William	52	Farmer	3
Baily, J. R.	60	Farmer	9

Baker, Charles	64	Brick mason	2
Barton, Abner	59	Farmer	5
Barton, Martin	35	Farmer	3
Bashaw, J. E.	49	Hotel keeper	2
Beachharg, B. N.	44	Blacksmith	2
Berry, J. W.	28	Merchant	1
Blackburn, J. H.	32	Farmer	1
Blanton, Wilkins	54	Merchant	1
Blanton, Willis	50	Farmer	11
Bowden, G. E.	41	Farmer	3
Brantley, James A.	52	Merchant	5
Brawley, C. C.	42	Farmer	5
Brewer, C. C.	30	Circuit Clerk	4
Brewer, John	47	Farmer	2
Briant, Abner	55	Farmer	5
Britton, M. D.	37	Farmer	6
Brixey, Joanna	43	Domestic	1
Brixey, Walton	55	Farmer	1
Brown, Ann	20	Domestic	6
Brown, May	54	Domestic	2
Brown, Red	45	Farmer	10
Brown, Robert	50	Farmer	5
Brown, S. H.	23	Farmer	3
Bryant, David	52	Farmer	2
Bryant, J. M.	48	Farmer	4
Bryant, M.	54	Farmer	10
Bryant, M. L.	35	Farmer	2
Buckner, W. B.	36	Farmer	8
Call, James	32	Farmer	2
Campbell, G. R.	30	Farmer	1

Carden, J. A.	30	Sheriff	1
Carden, Lewis	51	Farmer	1
Carden, M. A.	26	Farmer	2
Carden, Sarah	56	Domestic	2
Cargile, Granta	25	Farming	1
Carlile, J. M.	48	Farmer	4
Cash, John	65	Farmer	12
Chapman, G. W.	50	Blacksmith	4
Charles, J.	65	Farmer	9
Clark, Jas. A.	37	Farmer	2
Cole, Nancy	65	None	5
Coleman, (Coulston), C.	62	Farmer	1
Crabtree, Eli	29	Carpenter	2
Crawford, Joseph	62	CP Minister	2
Crocket, John	53	Farmer	6
Crockett, Samuel	51	Farmer	15
Cunningham, Eliza	49	None	15
Cunningham, Mark	57	Farmer	1
Cunningham, Martha	76	None	3
Cunningham, Rolly	62	Farmer	1
Cunningham, Thomas	47	Farmer	2
Daniel, Thos.	72	Carpenter	1
Davidson, D. V.	56	Farmer	5
Davidson, Hugh	65	Farmer	11
Davidson, J. H.	32	Farmer	3
Davidson, W. F.	37	Farmer	6
Davidson, Wm.	37	Farmer	1
Davis, A. B.	48	Doctor	15
Dickens, B. B.	63	Farmer	2
Dillard, L. F.	34	Farmer	2

Duncan, Daniel	22	Farmer	1
Easly, Rachel	58	Domestic	8
Edwards, G. W.	23	Merchant	1
Edwards, George	23	Brick maker	1
Elliott, Stephen	71	Farmer	8
Farrar, J. Z. A.	44	Farmer & Merchant	13
Farrar, Wm.	63	Farmer	4
Farris, I. F. L.	50	Farmer	4
Farris, J. F. L.	50	Farmer	7
Ferrill, R. R.	28	Liveryman	1
Finch, S. P.	53	Farmer	11
Finch, William H.	21	Clerk Store	2
Foster, H. A.	39	Farmer	1
Freeman, Obediah	68	Farmer	2
Green, Mary	59	Domestic	5
Green, R. H.	54	Farmer	1
Gunn, T. L.	51	Farmer	7
Hale, Sydney	58	Domestic	8
Hall, James W.	30	Farmer	4
Hampton, Ransome	52	Farmer	8
Hancock, M. L.	28	Farmer	2
Harris, Lewis	53	Blacksmith	1
Harris, William	50	Farmer	5
Hart, Moses	68	Farmer	1
Hazelwood, J. W.	36	Farmer	1
Hesk, A. W.	24	Farmer	2
Hickerson, Charles	41	Farmer	7
Hickerson, Joseph	34	Farmer	2
Hickerson, L. D	31	Farmer	10
Hickerson, Little	36	Merchant	2

Hickerson, Martha	76	None	1
Hickerson, W. A.	45	Farmer	9
Hickerson, Wily	43	Farmer	9
Hickerson, Wm. P.	42	Attorney-at-Law	8
Hill, J. J.	35	Farmer	3
Hill, Many	52	Farmer	3
Hines, W. J.	34	Farmer	13
Hitts, B.	41	Farmer	1
Hodge, Alex	55	Farmer	27
Hodge, John	75	Farmer	3
Holt, A. M.	56	Doctor	6
Houghton, E. H.	46	Farmer	4
How, Joseph	46	Farmer & Merchant	6
Howard, J. G.	26	Farmer	6
Huggins, W. S.	34	Merchant Mills	6
Jackson, G. W.	33	ME Minister	2
Jackson, T. H.	30	Meth. Minister	2
Jacob, Elizabeth	37	Farming	5
Jacob, Pleasant	57	Farmer	2
Jacobs, A.	41	Farmer	15
Jacobs, C. C.	36	Farmer	7
Jacobs, Rebecca	60	Farming	2
Jacobs, Starky	19	Farmer	2
Jacobs, Wm.	60	Farmer & Merchant	3
Jarnigan, S.	54	Farmer	1
Jarnigan, Uzzely	44	Farmer	4
Jarnigan, William	48	Farmer	1
Jenkins, B. F.	50	Farmer	14
Jenkins, Nancy	73	None	4
Johnson, John	58	Farmer	10

Jones, H. C.	26	Farmer	2
Jones, T. A.	48	Farmer	1
Judd, J. W.	48	Minister	1
Keele, J. W.	40	Farmer	2
Keele, Jacob	74	Farmer	13
Keeling, E.	57	Surveyor	1
Keeling, T. A.	24	Farmer	2
Kendall, Thomas S.	84	None	1
Kincannon, L. A.	51	Farmer	22
Knight, L. E.	29	Sawyer	1
Koger, James	60	Carpenter	6
Larence, James	49	Farmer	8
Larence, Tabitha	50	Domestic	8
Laseter, R. E.	43	Merchant	2
Law, Thomas H.	28	Farmer	1
Layne, Benjamin	52	Farmer	11
Layne, Wyatt	55	Farmer	13
Logan, James	41	Farmer	1
Lusk, Edward	39	Carpenter	4
Lusk, Isaac	69	Farmer	5
Manly, H. H.	41	Farmer	1
Marsh, J. W.	53	Farmer	3
Martin, L. C.	53	Farmer	1
Martin, William	46	Farmer	1
Maxwell, Andrew	52	Farmer	14
May, W. W.	34	Farmer	1
McCoy, James	49	Carpenter	1
McFerson, G. W.	70	Farmer	2
McGill, John	45	Farmer	15
McMany, W. A.	50	Farmer	6

McMichael Martha	70	None (Farmer's wife)	2
McMichael, Wm.	27	Farmer	2
McMichael, Wm., Sr.	55	Farmer	5
McQuiller (McQuidy), M.	43	Maunfacturer	2
Messick, Charley	57	Farmer	2
Messick, G. B.	41	Farmer	5
Miller, E. S.	40	Doctor	1
Miller, George	60	Farmer	12
Mines, W. J.	31	Sawyer	4
Mitchell, R. J.	36	Farmer	2
Moore, Alford	56	Farmer	10
Moore, B. F.	36	Farmer & Merchant	6
Moore, Mary	78	None	10
Moore, William	73	Farmer	1
Morgan, H.	61	Merchant	5
Morgan, W. C.	27	Merchant	1
Morrow, Samuel	41	Farmer	1
Neville, John	18	None	2
Neville, Lucy	49	Farming	2
Neville, Pleasant H.	53	Farmer	5
Neville, Polenina	40	Farming	10
Neville, Roy	29	Farmer	2
Nite, Lucinda	66	Domestic	12
Norton, Henry W.	100	None given	6
Norton, J. K.	53	Doctor	7
Norton, N. G.	52	Farmer	5
Norton, N. P.	40	Farmer	2
Norton, R. J. (Rufus)	23	Farmer	3
Norton, Wm.	60	Doctor	1
Parson (Pearson), J. E.	34	None	3

Parson (Person), Soloman	55	Farmer	1
Patton, John J.	43		3
Patton, Joseph	43	Minister	6
Payne, J. S.	50	Shoemaker	1
Penson, W. F.	36	Farmer	2
Petty, R. M.	47	Farmer	11
Phillips, Lorenzo D.	52	Farmer & Meth. Minister	4
Phillips, M. C.	49	Farmer	2
Phillips, Sarah	51	Domestic	1
Phillips, W. H.	39	Farmer	1
Phillips, Wm.	62	Farmer	2
Pittman, J. E.	35	ME Minister	3
Powell, Alex	74	Farmer	4
Powell, D. J.	30	Farmer	3
Powell, W. D.	38	Farmer	1
Powers, Thomas	63	Farmer	36
Powers, William	32	Farmer	5
Price, P. H.	47	Farmer	22
Price, R. J.	60	Farmer	7
Puckett, E. B.	46	Grammar Teacher	1
Pulley, Gideon	72	Farmer	12
Pulley, W. H.	36	Farmer	5
Putnam, W. W.	34	Farmer	18
Pyson, J. C.	52	Farmer	1
Ragan, Susan	59	Domestic	6
Ramsey, A. J.	34	Farmer	9
Randall, David	59	Farmer	15
Rankins, John	49	Farmer	3
Rayburn, French	27	Farmer	14
Rayburn, J. W. G. (James)	34	Farmer	8

Rayburn, R. D.	30	Farmer	5
Rayburn, W. K.	28	Farmer	1
Rayburn, William	28	Farmer	4
Reynolds, Elijah	30	Farmer	30
Reynolds, Frances	50	Domestic	6
Reynolds, J.	32	Carpenter	1
Rhodes, T. J.	56	Farmer	12
Rice, Septimus	52	Farmer	21
Richards, William	49	Farmer	1
Richardson, James	90	Farmer	1
Richardson, L. M.	39	Domestic (son – farmer)	5
Roach, William	35	Farmer	5
Roberts, J. T.	32	Farmer	2
Robertson, A. B.			3
Rodes, J. E.	31	Doctor	1
Rowland, Jacob	62	Farmer	12
Rucker, Benj.	28	Farmer	2
Sane, Thomas	36	Farmer	1
Savier, T. M.	37	Farmer	1
Sheid, H. S.	33	Farmer	4
Sheid, James M.	45	Farmer & Merchant	12
Sheid, Sarah	50	Domestic	3
Sheid, Sibel	81	None	6
Sherrill, Uriah	57	Bapt. Minister	7
Short, Joab	76	Farmer	7
Smith, J. C.	31	Farmer	3
Smith, J. M.	29	Farmer	5
Smith, Jeff	51	Farmer	2
Smith, Joe B.	31	Hotel	12
Snipes, J. W.	40	Farmer	1

Specke, Albert	38	Com. Laborer	1
Spuce, Thomas	61	Farmer	2
Starky, Cassander	40	Domestic	2
Starnes, W. P.	47	Farmer	1
Stevens, Ann Eliza	18	None	2
Stevens, E.	59	Farmer	1
Stevens, James W.	20	Farmer	2
Stevens, Jane	50	Farming	1
Stevens, John	23	Farmer	1
Stevenson, T. P.	62	Doctor and Farmer	5
Stewart, R.	39	Bookseller	1
Tarply, J. M.	29	Cab. Apprentice	2
Taylor, Elizabeth	67	Farming	4
Taylor, James	63	Bapt. Minister	11
Taylor, Robert	59	Farmer	5
Templeton, Jasper	32	Carpenter	1
Thoma, Peter	48	Farmer	1
Thompson, B. J.	26	Farmer	7
Tillman, Joseph	34	Farmer	2
Timmens, Anna	79	None	5
Turner, Elijah	47	Baptist Minister	6
Waite, W.	33	Farmer	4
Wakefield, J. H.	30	Farmer	1
Walker, Emily	19	None	2
Walker, Joseph	33	Farmer	2
Walker, Mary	59	Farmer	3
Walker, Robert	27	Farmer	7
Walker, Wm.	21	Farmer	2
Ward, B.	40	Bailiff	1
Warren, G.	34	Farmer	1

Waterson, Nancy	70	Farming	8
Waterson, Thomas	31	Farmer	4
Wileman, L.	47	Farmer	4
Wileman, L. R.	38	Farmer & Merchant	7
Wileman, Manly	59	Farmer	11
Wileman, William	42	Farmer	5
Wilkerson, J. M.	48	Farmer	12
Wilkerson, Wm. C.	44	Farmer	3
Williams, D. H.	57	Farmer	1
Willis, Elizabeth	62	Farming	20
Willis, Joseph	52	Farmer	4
Wilson, Jane	59	Farming	2
Wilson, Nancy	82	None	1
Wilson, Robert	55	Blacksmith	5
Wilson, T. W.	45	Farmer	1
Wilson, W. H.	32	Farmer	5
Winfrey, James	57	Farmer	1
Winton, J.	35	Farmer	2
Winton, John Jr.	35	Farmer	1
Winton, John Sr.	64	Farmer	17
Winton, Steven	67	Farmer	32
Winton, T. J.	24	Farmer	1
Woods, W. A.	33	Druggist	1
Yates, John	38	Farmer	3

"I think we must get rid of slavery or we must get rid of freedom."

~~Ralph Waldo Emerson

THE EMANCIPATION PROCLAMATION

The Emancipation Proclamation (page 1) Record Group 11 General Records of the United States. (Reprinted from the National Archives & Records Administration)

President Abraham Lincoln issued the Emancipation Proclamation on January 1, 1863, as the nation approached its third year of bloody civil war. The proclamation declared "that all persons held as slaves" within the rebellious states "are, and henceforward shall be free."

Despite this expansive wording, the Emancipation Proclamation was limited in many ways. It applied only to states that had seceded from the United States, leaving slavery untouched in the loyal border states. It also expressly exempted parts of the Confederacy (the Southern secessionist states) that had already come under Northern control. Most important, the freedom it promised depended upon Union (United States) military victory.

Although the Emancipation Proclamation did not end slavery in the nation, it captured the hearts and imagination of millions of Americans and fundamentally transformed the character of the war. After January 1, 1863, every advance of federal troops expanded the domain of freedom. Moreover, the Proclamation announced the acceptance of black men into the Union Army and Navy, enabling the liberated to become liberators. By the end of the war, almost 200,000 black soldiers and sailors had fought for the Union and freedom.

From the first days of the Civil War, slaves had acted to secure their own liberty. The Emancipation Proclamation confirmed their insistence that the war for the Union must become a war for freedom. It added moral force to the Union cause and strengthened the Union both militarily and politically. As a milestone along the road to slavery's final destruction, the Emancipation Proclamation has assumed a place among the great documents of human freedom.

The original of the Emancipation Proclamation of January 1, 1863, is in the National Archives in Washington, DC. With the text covering five pages the document was originally tied with narrow red and blue ribbons, which were attached to the signature page by an impression of the seal of the United States. Most of the ribbon remains; parts of the seal are still decipherable, but other parts have worn off.

The document was bound with other proclamations in a large volume preserved for many years by the Department of State. When it was prepared for binding, it was reinforced with strips along the center folds and then mounted on a still larger sheet of heavy paper. Written in red ink on the upper right-hand corner of this large sheet is the number of the Proclamation, 95, given to it by the Department of State long after it was signed. With other records, the volume containing the Emancipation Proclamation was transferred in 1936 from the Department of State to the National Archives of the United States.

CELEBRATING EMANCIPATION

Eighth of August Jubilee

Although Lincoln signed the Emancipation Proclamation on January 1, 1863, the blacks in Tennessee chose to recognize the eighth day of August to celebrate their day of freedom. Why August 8th? Some speculate it is because this was the date that Tennessee Military Governor, and later U. S. President, Andrew Johnson, freed his personal slaves in 1863, at his Greenville, Tennessee farm. Others allege that enslaved people in Tennessee and Kentucky didn't learn of the Emancipation Proclamation until August 8, 1863. Regardless of its origins, the 8th of August, according to Clarksville historian Dr. Nancy J. Dawson, "offered black people in the segregated South a place to be free together, especially from white racism."

Andrew Johnson's former slave, Sam, was instrumental in creating the first August 8th celebrations. The Knoxville Chronicle dated August 9th, 1871 reported an August 8th celebration in Greenville, TN as the first known August 8th event. Andrew Johnson is said to have attended the celebration. The day was marked with a parade, speeches and picnics. Attendees played games and danced to lively tunes

The August celebration became known as the "Eighth of August Jubilee" (Fourth of August in Manchester) and continues to be recognized as a holiday in the African-American community in Tennessee and surrounding states. In 2007, Tennessee Governor Phil Bredesen signed legislation (House Bill No. 207) acknowledging August 8th as "Emancipation Day" in the state... "... to honor and recognize the celebration of the action of Andrew Johnson, seventeenth president of the United States and then military governor of Tennessee, in freeing his personal slaves on August 8, 1863, and the significance of emancipation in the history of Tennessee."

JUNETEENTH

Juneteenth is another day of celebration commemorating the June 19, 1865 announcement of the abolition of slavery in the U.S. State of Texas, and probably the oldest. Dating back to 1865, it was on June 19th that the Union soldiers announced that the war had ended and that the enslaved were now free. (Note that this was two and a half years <u>after</u> President Lincoln's Emancipation Proclamation (which had become official January 1, 1863.) Much like the Eighth of August Jubilee, Juneteenth is celebrated across the south with programs and festivals commemorating the African-American Liberation.

"I didn't know I was a slave until I found out I couldn't do the things I wanted."
~~Frederick Douglass

U.S. BUREAU OF REFUGEES, FREEDMEN, AND ABANDONED LANDS

(More commonly known as The Freedmen's Bureau)

The Freedmen's Bureau, more formally known as the Bureau of Refugees, Freedmen and Abandoned Lands, was established by an Act of Congress on March 3, 1865, two months before the end of the Civil War. The government recognized that the former slaves would need assistance with housing, food, jobs and medical aid. Intended as a temporary agency to last the duration of the war plus one year, the bureau was placed under the authority of the War Department and the majority of its original employees were Civil War soldiers. The Bureau established churches and schools in the south, and offered legal assistance. They strived to reunite families separated under slavery.

Until the 13th and 14th amendments were passed in 1866, the former slaves were not considered citizens and were not sure what to call themselves. Preferring not to be called ex-slaves or former slaves they settled on the title of Freedmen.

General Clinton B. Fisk was appointed to head up the division of the Bureau that covered Kentucky, Tennessee and Northern Alabama. In January 1866, Fisk organized a school for freedmen in Nashville. A year later the school became Fisk University and offered a program to train black teachers for the Freedmen's schools.

While the Freedmen's Bureau worked hard in assisting the ex-slaves in locating jobs, housing, and food and organizing hospitals, orphanages and homes for the elderly, and teaching them how to manage their finances, many white citizens opposed the Bureau's actions and the freeing of the slaves and there were many confrontations between the races. While the Bureau didn't always succeed at its endeavors it was successful in its educational goals

REPORTS FROM THE FREEDMEN'S BUREAU

Freedmen's Bureau List of Outrages Perpetrated by the Whites Upon the Freedmen in the State of Tennessee from April 1865 to March 1866

Joel B. Smith, Supt for *Coffee Co*, reports
Aug 1st "The Freedmen of this county are industriously engaged in their avocation of business and are undisturbed in their guaranteed rights and privileges, there are a few poor and infirm Freedmen at this place the county court has been notified of their condition and at their last regular meeting appointed suitable committees to locate a site for the building of a Poor House for the use and benefit of poor Freedmen of the County."
http://www.freedmensbureau.com/tennessee/reports/tennreport.htm

County: Coffee.*Assailants* Three white men unknown. *Injured*: **Zarey Ordman**. *Date*: Dec 1866. *Nature of attack*: Beat & shot at. *Comments*: No clue whatever as to the identity of the guilty party.

County: Coffee. *Assailants:* Young white men unknown. *Injured*: **Ann Whittaker** & **Julia Oats**. *Date*: January 1867. *Nature of attack*: Tore down house. *Comments*: Some of the guilty party were arrested but acquitted.
http://www.freedmensbureau.com/tennessee/outrages/tennoutrages1.htm

County: Coffee.*Assailants:* **James Taylor** & others.*Injured*: Freedmen.*Date*: January 1867.*Nature of attack*: Shooting. *Comments*: Taylor fled & no steps taken by the civil authorities for his arrest.
http://www.freedmensbureau.com/tennessee/outrages/tennoutrages2.htm

Coffee Co. reports a freedman by the name of **Pinkney Brannon**, who was driven from home, his life being threatened.

On the night of Dec.11 the Freedmen's school house was burned by incendiaries. Numerous instances occur in which unprincipled white men have taken advantage of the ignorance & confidence of the freedmen & swindled them out of all their hard-earned wages.
http://www.freedmensbureau.com/tennessee/outrages/tennoutrages1.htm

Mr. **S. Stevens** McMinnville, Tenn. December 11, 1865 states that during divine service a colored woman entered the church. A **Mr. Pennibarker** asked the preacher to stop – and ordered all colored folks to leave – no one left – at close of the service Mr. Pennibarker stopped the colored woman at the door and chastised her severely.
http://www.freedmensbureau.com/tennessee/outrages/tennoutrages1.htm

Mr. **R. Caldwell,** Supt. *Pulaski, Tenn*. Reports January 19, that in several instances he has secured considerable amounts
to colored laborers – which they would have lost but for his efforts.
http://www.freedmensbureau.com/tennessee/outrages/tennoutrages1.htm

SEGREGATION

(Free but not equal)

The Tennessee Constitution of 1870, Article XI, Section 12 states "No school established or aided under this section shall allow white and negro children to be received as scholars together in the same school."

Therefore, several Colored Schools were established in Coffee County:

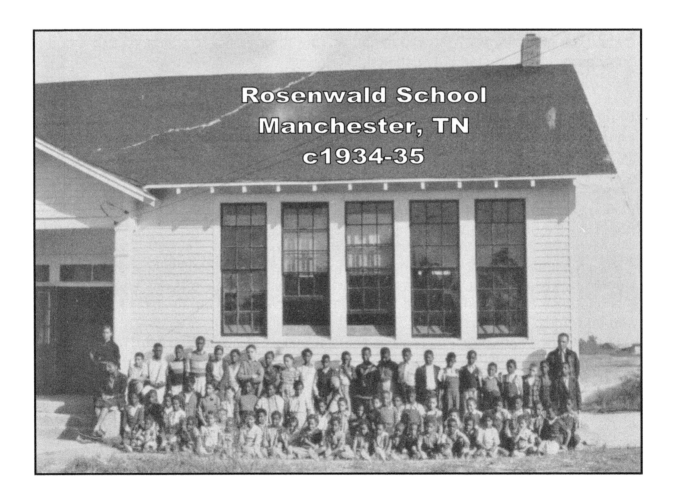

Rosenwald School. Julius Rosenwald, an American businessman and Philanthropist was responsible for establishing a Fund for the educating of colored children. He provided millions of dollars in matching funds to set up schools across the south. Manchester's Rosenwald school was located on Rye Street.

Rosenwald School Children, 1933 or 1934

1. Northcutt, Henry, Jr. (June)
2. Northcutt, J. W.
3. Vannoy, Hershel
4. Vannoy, Herman (Dude)
5.
6. Northcutt, S. P.
7. Hickerson, William Hence (Bill)
8. Royal, Samuel (Sambo);
9. Walker, Alonzo (1st black Alderman here)
10. Adams, Norman
11. Vannoy, Esther

12. Keele, Nell
13. Montgomery, Frances ??
14.
15. Ramsey, Sammie Mae Jackson's mother)
16. McGee, Razzie Lee
17. Montgomery, Elizabeth (Samuel L.
18. Hickerson, Lorene (McReynolds – provided picture)
19. Tubbs, Cecelia
20. Tubbs, Harold
21. McGee, Doris
22. Maupins, Will M.
23. Vannoy, Juanita
24. Brown, Jean
25. Maupins, Mary
26. Lane, Earldene
27. Murray, Brent
28. Newsome, Nathan (son of Charlie – Early UPS/FedEx –picked up freight from train and delivered
29. Winton, A. J.
30. Hopkins, Algie – Teacher (from Brownsville, TN)

"As early as 1863, the U.S. Army began to provide housing, food and schools for the formerly enslaved refugees who came into their lines" states Dr. Michael Bradley, local historian and author. However, it wasn't until the Freedmen's Bureau was established in March 1865 that the school was built. Rosenwald was a K-8th grade school and Algee Hopson was principal. Some of the teachers were John Malone, Beatrice Riche, Mr. Harris and Ms. Whitaker. Lunch was served to the students and Hazel Hill was the cook.

When the Supreme Court ruled that black students could attend white schools, Rosenwald School closed and the building was divided and moved to a location on Kefauver Street behind the People's Bank. It was turned into apartments.

Rosenwald "School" as it looks today. It was moved and converted into Apartments.

Davidson Academy Dr. Michael Bradley reports that the Freedmen's School in Tullahoma, was actually built in 1864 and was part of a refugee settlement of "small shacks," as described by a U.S. Army officer, in the area where the C.D. Stamps Community Center now stands on South Jackson Street. The Freedmen schools were built of wood and they were burned down and rebuilt several times.

COLORED SCHOOL, TULLAHOMA, TENN.

Davidson Academy
Photo located and provided by Marjorie Collier
Page 10 of The N. C. & St. L. RR. NEWS ITEM, May 15, 1929 and
Page 9 of Tullahoma Time-Table, April 1991

In the 1920s the Tullahoma Negro School was established for the education of colored students. Its name was changed to the Davidson Academy in 1920. It was a Rosenwald School. The county, by contract with the Tullahoma City School Board, agreed to pay the salary of the principal, Professor C. D. Stamps.

Davidson Academy Girl's Exercise Class

Front row, from left to right: Helen Cunningham, Treavor Mitchell, Betty Sue Hickerson (Adams), Willie Mae Maupins (Crutchfield), Lydia Biles, and Della Sims. In the back row from left: Professor G. W. Hall, Mammie Ashley, Ann Duncan, Lorene Hickerson (McReynolds), Eunice Cunningham (Moore), Ada Lee, Gloria Smartt and Jennie Adams.

Other Black Schools in the County

(Heritage of Coffee County; submitted by Marie Hatfield)

Cole Ridge School was near Noah in 1919. There is no further record of the teachers there.

Hurricane School was near the Calhoun School near Hwy. 41N. In 1909, T. A. Keeling was teaching there and in 1936 John Malone was the teacher.

Patton's Chapel School was located between Calls and Prairie Plains. Beatrice Riche taught there in 1936. Henry Riche, Rosie Lee Wooten and Beatrice Riche taught there in the 1940s. The school closed in 1949.

Samonia School was located between Hillsboro and Prairie Plains. The earliest teacher recorded was Allie Brown in 1919. Later teachers were: Ora Murray, Christine Maulin, Beatrice Riche, and Henry Riche. The school closed in 1936.

Smith's Chapel School location is unknown. However, Leighton Ewell lists the school in his book, "History of Coffee County" as being in session in 1936-1938. The teachers were: Loris Acklin and Delsie Whittaker.

Summitville School was a one-room school located near Hwy. 55. It was operating in 1935-1936 with Elizabeth Shedd as the teacher. Other teachers were: Elizabeth Wooten, Beatrice Riche and Mattie Politto. (From "The Summitville Story.") The school closed in 1963 and students went to East Coffee Elementary and Coffee County Jr. High School.

Riverview School was located in Manchester. It opened after Rosenwald school closed in 1957. Riverview closed in 1964. The school was located on Emerson Street. It was a three-teacher school at one time. When the schools were integrated the children went to Manchester City Schools. The building was then used as the Alternative School for the Coffee County School system. It is now closed.

Mr. Allen Kincannon was the principal of Riverview for many years. Some other teachers at Riverview were: Mrs. Elizabeth Wooten, A. H. Harris and Beatrice Riche.

Bus Drivers were: Hiram Miller and M. W. Hickerson, Sr.

The MANCHESTER TIMES

Blacks Have Proud Role in Coffee County History

By Mike Garrison

(Reprinted from the Manchester Times, Thursday Morning, July 8, 1976)

Manchester and rural Coffee County's relatively small black community was forced to build its own schools, find its economic support as best it could, build its own churches, and establish its own traditions.

The small group has progressed but still looks back at its leaders since the first blacks arrived in Coffee County prior to the Civil War.

Mrs. Beatrice Riche, a retired school teacher, found these historical facts through extensive research:

Blacks in Manchester largely attend three Christian denominations – Church of Christ, Methodist and Missionary Baptist.

Will Vannoy and his wife, Ella, gave the grounds for the first Church of Christ building on Lane Street. The Vannoys called Marshall Newsom of Viola to serve as minister. Mr. Newsom's son, Charlie, was chosen as his assistant.

That church building served the congregation until about 1950 when a new building and edifice were built.

The Will Vannoy family, the Newsom family, Tubbs family and others were among the first to worship at the Lane Street Church.

Stephen Chapel Methodist was organized by John Naunce and supported in its infancy by such members as Robert L. Vannoy, Matilda Vannoy and Lillie Vannoy. Later church leaders included Joe Northcutt, Elisha Sandridge, Thola Winton, Iola Johnson, E. Murray, S. Estell and W. Walker.

The last church to be organized in Manchester's black community is First Missionary Baptist Church on Raven Street. The congregation was formed 45 years ago mainly through the efforts of Mrs. Hattie Walker and her daughter, Jessie.

The building was erected under the leadership of the Rev. L. W. Windham of South Pittsburg and later remodeled under the leadership of the Rev. W. A. Pryor, the current pastor.

Some members of the church have been Daisy Winton, Lizzie Brown, Christine Mayfield and Josephine Joyce.

Summitville's black community attends four churches – Church of Christ, Methodist, Baptist and Methodist Episcopal. Mrs. Carrie Lee Etter was a Church of Christ leader and also a talented midwife. She attended the late Dr. Womack for many years.

Ida Lillie Stephenson was of the Methodist Episcopal faith. There was no church building for that faith but different groups held services in the school building.

Mrs. Rosena Wooten and her daughter Lottie were influential in Methodist church work. Ethel Macon and Bob Lee represented the Baptist faith.

First Preacher?

Paul Elam of the Elamtown Community near Summitville is thought to be the first and only black minister born and reared around Manchester. He preaches today at Green Meadow Church of Christ at Fosterville in Bedford County.

Legend has it that blacks once buried their dead in Manchester's white cemetery. For some reason town leaders raised money and organized a separate cemetery for blacks on the south side of town, which is still the location of the black cemetery.

Blacks were given the option of burying their dead at this site or in lots on Hillsboro Highway. The highway site, however, was heavily wooded and was not used.

Ben Patton was a leader of the black community at Prairie Plains. A large estate owner, Mr. Patton, donated land and logs shortly after Emancipation for the building of a church and school. Mr. Patton was thought to have been the wealthiest black in the county and left large farms to each of his daughters at the time of his death.

Henry Clepper, great-grandfather of Mrs. Beatrice Riche and Mrs. Elizabeth Wooten, is said to have used his team of oxen to pull Mr. Patton's logs to the construction site of the building.

According to Legend, Mr. Patton housed a school teacher who was sent to Prairie Plains to assist in putting on an Emancipation celebration on Sept 22. Blacks in the area celebrated by marching with flags and singing songs about freedom.

That night Mr. Patton and the teacher were awakened by hooded men who took the two black leaders outside and assaulted them. The teacher left soon afterwards.

For many years the education of black children meant hours of daily travel. There were no high schools for blacks in Coffee County, the closest being in Winchester.

Henry Riche drove his A-Model to that school daily and decided in 1932 that he would use his vehicle as a school bus for Coffee County blacks. Mr. Riche would begin his run early each morning, making stops in Prairie Plains, Summitville, Manchester and places throughout the county.

Pay with Produce

He was paid with produce from black farmers but this did little to help Mr. Riche with supplying gasoline. Finally, Basil McMahan, then Manchester's school superintendent began giving Mr. Riche a monthly check of $6 to help with the gas. Later Sam Wooten took over the bus-driving chores as the cost still was too expensive for Mr. Riche to continue.

Mrs. Elizabeth Wooten was the first and only black teacher in the Manchester school system. Other pioneer black teachers are Miss Ella Vannoy, Miss Elizabeth S. Newsom, Miss Clara Vannoy, Miss Margie Walker, Mrs. Lura Wooten Webb, Mrs. Louella Elliot Darwin, Mrs. Beatrice Riche and Henry Riche.

Robert Vannoy was a prosperous construction worker and inventor in the black community. He had his own brick kiln in Manchester where he made and sold his bricks. Mr. Vannoy could read blueprints and was skilled at laying bricks. He helped build many homes in Manchester, Nashville and the Midstate area.

Mr. Vannoy invented a folding ironing board and was known to be a "good liver." He had a large family and educated his children at Walden University in Nashville.

Mr. Vannoy was the son of a white slave-holder and a mother of mixed blood. The first Manchester black to have a telephone in his own home, he was reluctant to make a show of what he owned because of the feelings of whites at that time about the prosperity of the black race.

He came to own much property, but his wife was dispossessed of the land after his death through mysterious means.

Starts Celebration

Linday Brewer was the man responsible for the famous Fourth of August celebration which is still held. Mr. Brewer was told he could not sell ice cream from his restaurant at the corner of East Main and North Spring Streets on the Fourth of July because whites intended to sell ice cream on the Courthouse lawn.

"All right," he said, "I'll just sell my ice cream on the Fourth of August." The Celebration became a tradition after that day about 100 years ago. Today the Fourth of August is a time of dancing, merriment and homecoming.

The festivals at one time stretched over a three-day period but now lasts only one day since both men and women are employed.

DESEGREGATION

From Basil McMahan's "Coffee County Then and Now"

The year 1964 was a landmark year in several ways. Before this year white and colored students had attended different schools. The County and City schools officials combined in public resolutions which opened all County and City schools to all pupils regardless of race, creed, or color based upon the recent U.S. Supreme Court decisions and "Bill of Civil Rights." In August the Riverview School opened with Allen Kincannon as principal and teacher and Mrs. Elizabeth Wooten as assistant. They were immediately transferred to white schools. Mr. Kincannon to the Coffee County Junior High School and Mrs. Wooten to Manchester College Street School. She was an outstanding first grade teacher for several years until her retirement. [page 148]

In 1964 the high school section of Davidson Academy was discontinued. The ninth-grade students went to West Junior High and the top three grades to the High School. Grades seven and eight were discontinued in the fall of 1965 and desegregation of the faculty was begun in the fall of 1966. Davidson Academy, which had begun as an all-black school, was used for sixth grade, special education classes, and a kindergarten class. [page 204]

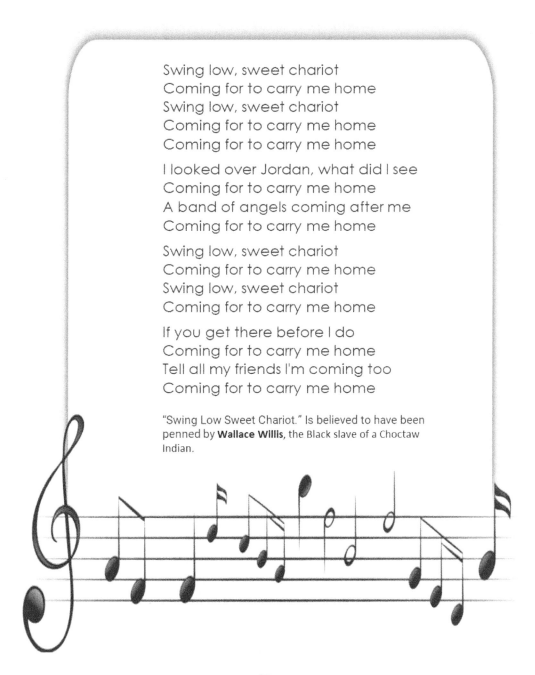

Swing low, sweet chariot
Coming for to carry me home
Swing low, sweet chariot
Coming for to carry me home
Coming for to carry me home

I looked over Jordan, what did I see
Coming for to carry me home
A band of angels coming after me
Coming for to carry me home

Swing low, sweet chariot
Coming for to carry me home
Swing low, sweet chariot
Coming for to carry me home

If you get there before I do
Coming for to carry me home
Tell all my friends I'm coming too
Coming for to carry me home

"Swing Low Sweet Chariot." Is believed to have been penned by **Wallace Willis**, the Black slave of a Choctaw Indian.

AFTER THE WAR

The 1870 census showed that 1,392 blacks remained in the county. While farming still remained the number one profession, it is interesting to see on the census how there are 3 different divisions of farming. There were 104 "farm laborers," 19 "farmers," and 7 that were in "farming." Eighty-four occupations were listed as 'laborer.' Laborer may or may not have been farm work. Other occupations listed were: 4 at home, 1 barber, 1 carpenter, 8 blacksmiths, 1 distillery worker, 18 cooks, 5 cooks and washers, 4 washers, 40 domestic servants, 1 preacher, 13 rail road workers, 2 sawmill workers, 1 paper mill worker, 1 porter, 1 woodcutter, 1 shoe maker, 1 stone mason, 1 workman, 1 teamster, 1 school teacher, 45 housekeepers, 13 servants, and 60 listed as none, or unknown.

Below is a list of the Negroes remaining in Coffee County, their ages and their occupations. Just the heads of household are given. Children who are listed were living in a white household.

Blacks listed in the 1870 Census:

Name of Head	Age	Occupation
Allen, Barb	23	Domestic Servant
Allen, Mary	19	Washer
Alley, Henry	22	Farm Laborer
Alley, Jack	60	Farm Laborer
Anderson, Marah	30	Domestic Servant
Armstrong, Jason	51	Farm Laborer
Armstrong, Tip	52	Farm Laborer
Armstrong, Tipton	48	Farm Laborer
Arnold, Ann	35	Keeping House
Arnold, Hannah	50	Domestic Servant

Ashley, Jane	9	None
Ashley, Mark	21	Farm Laborer
Ashley, Mc	37	Farm Laborer
Ashley, Millie	35	Domestic Servant
Ashley, Perry	60	Domestic Servant
Ashley, Willis	46	Stone Mason
Austell, James	19	Farm Laborer
Austill, Silas	7	None
Austille, Charles	50	Laborer
Austille, Sam	15	None
Bailey, Elizabeth	20	Keeping House
Baily, Jesse	50	Keeping House
Barner, Charles	40	Laborer on RR
Barnes, William	19	Framing
Batie, John	36	Farm Laborer
Beaty, Anthony	45	Laborer
Bell, William	9	None
Biddle, Eliza	24	Cook & Washer
Bishop, Sam	33	Farmer
Blair, Nathan	25	Farm Laborer
Blair, Samuel	26	Farm Laborer
Blanton, John	55	Farm Laborer
Blanton, Thadious	50	Carpenter
Bobo, Susy	15	None
Bough, George	56	Laborer
Bowden, Elaine	8	None
Bowen, Adaline	35	None
Bowen, Frank	62	Farming
Brenn, Rhodes	25	Paper Mill Worker
Brewer, Sam	33	Laborer

Brier, Susan	13	Domestic Servant
Brighton, Idia	45	Keeping House
Broils, Meriah	45	Domestic Servant
Broker, James	65	Farm Laborer
Brown, Anthony	17	Laborer
Brown, Emaline	26	Cook at Hotel
Brown, Monroe	17	Farm Laborer
Brown, Nancy	35	Cook
Brown, Thomas	40	Farmer
Bryan, Mary	56	Cook & Washer
Bryant, Joseph	34	None
Bryant, Mary	54	Keeping House
Burress, Samuel	33	Farm Laborer
Cardin, Adam	80	Farm Laborer
Cardin, Allice	14	None
Cardin, Peter	38	Farm Laborer
Caulson, Isaac	59	Laborer
Chafin, Morris	67	Laborer
Chafin, Pleasant	51	Laborer
Chapman, Clarissa	47	None
Charles, Josephine	12	None
Clark, George	25	Laborer
Clark, Warren	50	Farm Laborer
Clepee, Humphrey	23	Farmer
Coffman, Boker	65	Farm Laborer
Cole, Charlotte	35	Washer
Colley, Martha	45	Domestic Servant
Colly, Martha	17	Domestic Servant
Cook, Peter	50	Blacksmith
Cook, Sarah	15	House Servant

Cotner, Alexander	21	Farm Laborer
Cotner, Sallie	40	Keeping House
Cotner, Sophia	58	Keeping House
Crockertt, Kitty	23	Keeping House
Crocket, Amba	15	None
Crocket, Isaac	54	Laborer
Crockett, George	40	Laborer
Crockett, Harry	56	Farm Laborer
Crockett, Isaac	50	Laborer
Cunningham, A.	38	Laborer
Cunningham, Anthony	72	Laborer
Cunningham, Eliza	59	Keeping House
Cunningham, Jack	42	Laborer
Cunningham, Jinsey	53	Keeping House
Cunningham, Mary	70	None
Cunningham, William	17	Servant
Daniel, Rosa	17	Cook
Danse, Mose	70	Farm Laborer
Darolly, John	35	Farm Laborer
Davidson, Alexander	22	Farm Laborer
Davidson, Charlott	48	Domestic Servant
Davidson, Martha	11	House Servant
Davis, Adaline	15	None
Davis, Mary	22	House Servant
Davis, Matt	54	Laborer
Davis, Sam	55	Farm Laborer
Davis, William	26	Farmer
Derrin, David	29	Laborer
Dillard, Bucher	40	Blacksmith
Dillard, John	35	Farm Laborer

Diser, Harry	22	Farm Laborer
Dolby, Charles	10	None
Douglass, William	22	Teamster
Duff, Patrick	50	Laborer
Durley, Willis	27	Farming
Easley, Jefferson	25	Farm Laborer
Edwards, Vinson	85	Laborer
Elliot, Robert	18	Sawmill Worker
Elliott, John	6	None
Emerson, Nellie	35	Domestic Servant
Emerson, Pathene	14	Domestic Servant
Emery, Wileman	21	Farm Laborer
Estill, Sophia	70	Keeping House
Everett, Isaac	32	Laborer
Farrar, Emily	54	Keeping House
Fay, Richmond	25	Farm Laborer
Fields, Sam	52	Laborer
Finch, Charlotte	10	None
Finch, Martha	22	Domestic Servant
Finch, Wesley	26	Farm Laborer
Fletcher, America	37	Keeping House
Forester, Archy	20	Farm Laborer
Foster, Falio	101	Domestic Servant
Foster, John	33	None
Ganaway, Alice	13	Domestic Servant
Garrett, Delila	45	Cook
Gearneky, Thomas	14	None
Gilliam, David	60	Laborer
Grant, Lere	55	Farm Laborer
Gray, George	26	Laborer on RR

Green, John	45	Farm Laborer
Green, Washington	21	Farm Laborer
Gunn, Hannah	70	None
Gwinn, William	65	Laborer
Gwynn, William	65	Laborer
Haig, James	30	Farm Laborer
Hale, Andrew	61	Farmer
Hale, David	23	None
Hall, Elizabeth	16	Domestic Servant
Hall, William	60	Farm Laborer
Hamins, Matthew	56	Farmer
Hammins, Arrington	62	Farmer
Hanley, Alfred	48	None
Hardin, Oliver	36	Laborer
Harp, Esther	36	None
Harrison, Raybon	60	Farm Laborer
Heard, Chanda	22	Keeping House
Hickerson, Henry	41	Farm Laborer
Hickerson, Isabell	85	Domestic Servant
Hickerson, Matilda	56	At Home
Higason, Yance	65	Farm Laborer
Hill, Abram	44	Laborer
Hill, Alexander	35	Laborer
Hill, George	33	Laborer
Hill, Susan	43	Cook
Hitts, Nelson	17	Laborer
Holt, Edith	22	Domestic Servant
Holt, Matilda	15	None
Howard, Alfred	40	Farmer
Howard, Richard	30	Farm Laborer

Howe, Samuel	40	Farm Laborer
Innesford, Henry	36	Farm Laborer
Intel, John	58	Farm Laborer
Jackson, Sallie	23	House Servant
Jacob, David	37	Farmer
Jacobs, Emma	35	Domestic Servant
Jacobs, Henry	30	Farmer
Jacobs, Henry	35	Farm Laborer
Jacobs, James	30	Farm Laborer
Jacobs, James	38	Farmer
James, Samuel	92	None
James, Sandy	35	Laborer
Jenkins, Alice	12	Cook
Jenkins, Matilda	18	House Servant
Jenkins, Payton	41	Laborer on RR
Johnston, Tillman	40	Farm Laborer
Jonegan, Adam	21	Farm Laborer
Jones, Henry	25	Farm Laborer
Jones, Henry	28	Farm Laborer
Jones, Spencer	13	None
Jones, Thomas	63	Laborer
Kearney, George	57	Farm Laborer
Kearney, Monday	60	Farm Laborer
Keel, Polley	45	Cook
Keel, Thomas	35	Farm Laborer
Keele, George	35	Farm Laborer
Keele, George	75	Farm Laborer
Kelso, Violet	36	Cook
Kenley, John	27	Laborer
Kennerly, Ben	27	None

Kincannon, William	16	Laborer
Kincanon, Emma	23	Domestic Servant
Kincanon, Gatsey	23	Domestic Servant
Kincanon, James	21	Farm Laborer
King, Hannah	11	Cook
King, Sallie	40	Cook
King, Washington	25	Farm Laborer
Kinkannon, Arthur	25	Farm Laborer
Kinkanon, Henry	70	Farm Laborer
Knights, Muriane	12	None
Lane, Anderson	60	Farm Laborer
Lane, David	27	Farm Laborer
Lane, David	28	Farm Laborer
Lane, Gabriel	49	Laborer
Lane, John	47	Farm Laborer
Lane, Jondie	30	Keeping House
Layne, Calvin	36	Farming
Layne, Jacob	41	Laborer
Layne, Siloa	38	None
Lester, Clahmore	29	Laborer on RR
Luper, Eliza	50	Keeping House
Lyons, Frank	33	Farm Laborer
Lyons, Grant	28	Blacksmith
Lyons, Henry	25	Blacksmith
Marone, Charles	50	Laborer on RR
Marshall, Esther	21	Cook
Martin, Robison	50	Farm Laborer
Mason, Dread	70	Farmer
Mason, Ephraim	23	Farmer
Maxwell, Samuel	25	Farm Laborer

McCutchen, Sawer	40	Laborer
McGee, Robert	25	Laborer on RR
McMichael, Frankey	50	Keeping House
McMichael, Franky	45	Keeping House
Mears, Charles	45	Farmer
Messic, Julie	13	None
Meyerson, Eli	51	Farm Laborer
Moore, Henry	23	Laborer on RR
Moore, Louisa	45	Keeping House
Moore, Nelly	42	Domestic Servant
Mopin, Abner	60	Farm Laborer
Mosley, Julia	55	Keeping House
Mosley, Kenny	25	Farm Laborer
Mosley, Kinney	24	Farm Laborer
Mosley, Sally	20	Domestic Servant
Murphy, Robert	40	Farm Laborer, Preacher
Myers, Francis	38	Keeping House
Neal, Jerry	68	Farmer
Nelson, Solomon	95	Farm Laborer
Nevill, George	18	Laborer
Nevill, Hampton	55	Farmer
Nevill, Lucinda	67	Keeping House
Nevill, Sandy	65	Laborer
Neville, Anthony	36	Farmer
Noon, James	25	Laborer
Norell, Dolly	25	Wash Woman
Norton, Henderson	60	Farm Laborer
Norton, Lucinda	47	None
Norton, Margaret	16	Cook
Oaf, Julia	30	Keeping House

Ogleby, Dinah	23	House Servant
Olum, Zo	67	Farming
Osburn, Lavinia	27	Domestic Servant
Oscal, Adam	14	Servant
Parkinson, Alfred	30	Workman
Paskett, Bob	26	Laborer on RR
Paten, Margaret	70	Keeping House
Patten, Andrew	35	Farm Laborer
Patten, Henry	25	Farm Laborer
Patten, John	20	Farm Laborer
Patton, Andrew	23	None
Patton, Benjamin	57	Laborer
Patton, Henry	26	Farm Laborer
Patton, Isaac	31	Laborer
Patton, James	55	Laborer
Patton, Jeff	28	Laborer
Patton, John	20	Farm Laborer
Patton, Lavina	25	None
Patton, Lewis	28	Laborer
Patton, Maranda	24	Keeping House
Patton, Mariah	50	Keeping House
Patton, Mary	43	Keeping House
Pearson, Adaline	56	None
Pearson, Henry	38	Laborer on RR
Perkins, Jack	34	Laborer
Perkins, Tereace	50	Domestic Servant
Petty, Mary	34	Keeping House
Petty, Sarah	45	Washer
Philips, Jack	33	Laborer
Powers, Charles	30	Farm Laborer

Powers, Francis	30	Domestic Servant
Powers, Moses	45	Farm Laborer
Powers, Samuel	45	Farm Laborer
Powers, Vence	50	Keeping House
Preston, John	33	Laborer
Price, Emily	14	House Servant
Price, John	20	Blacksmith
Price, Sam	25	Laborer
Price, Samuel	20	Farm Laborer
Prince, Andrew	28	Laborer
Pruitt, Isaac	18	Farm Laborer
Pruitt, Rose	70	At Home
Pruitt, Thomas	50	Farm Laborer
Ragsdale, Mariah	56	None
Ramsey, Annah	57	None
Ramsey, Carroll	24	Laborer
Ramsey, William	35	Laborer
Rayborn, Jennie	60	Keeping House
Raywood, Nancy	31	Domestic Servant
Reagin, Celia	25	Farm Laborer
Reagin, Charlotte	44	Keeping House
Reagin, Mary	19	Farm Laborer
Reagin, Rozetta	56	Keeping House
Rhodes, Marion	11	None
Rice, Flem	30	Laborer
Rice, Nelson	30	Laborer
Rich, Allice	16	Domestic Servant
Rich, Amy	70	At home
Rich, Samuel	36	Woodcutter
Richards, Mary	35	Cook

Ring, Mariah	15	House Servant
Roades, Lavina	12	None
Roads, Moses	49	Laborer
Roads, Rebecca	55	Keeping House
Roads, Sallie	59	None
Roads, Vance	15	Laborer
Roberts, Jane	30	Keeping House
Robertson, Narcissa	17	Teaching School
Robison, Hezekiah	40	Farm Laborer
Robison, Marie	36	Domestic Servant
Rodgers, Harriet	35	Domestic Servant
Roton, William	22	Cook on R.R.
Row, Amanda	27	Keeping House
Row, Robert	40	Blacksmith
Rummels, John	42	Laborer
Runnels, Nonimus	73	Farming
Runnels, Paul	29	Laborer
Runnels, Phillip	39	Laborer
Ruskin, Calvin	42	Laborer
Russell, Martha	30	Cook & Washer
Russell, Robert	29	Laborer on RR
Rutledge, Cuffee	47	Laborer
Rutledge, James	27	Laborer
Rutledge, William	38	Laborer
Sanders, Abram	72	Farm Laborer
Sanders, Chemny	55	None
Savage, Thomas	14	Laborer
Savage, Thomas	50	Farmer
Scott, Betsy	70	Keeping House
Scott, Charlott	50	Keeping House

Scott, Harriet	26	None
Scott, Hulda	48	Farm Laborer
Scott, William	26	Farm Laborer
Scrub, Pleasant	42	Farm Laborer
Scruggs, Ann	22	Domestic Servant
Scruggs, Pleasant	35	Farm Laborer
Shafner, John	30	Laborer on RR
Shaw, Caroline	15	Domestic Servant
Sherrill, Mariah	15	None
Shofner, Amy	28	Keeping House
Shofner, Mary	52	Cook
Simmons, George	40	Laborer
Simms, Moriah	50	Keeping House
Smith, Charlotte	67	None
Smith, Elizabeth	27	At Home
Smith, John	25	Laborer
Smith, Millie	70	Keeping House
Smith, Sam	23	Laborer
Snore, Martha	40	Domestic Servant
Snore, Wilson	18	Domestic Servant
Spurlock, Nelson	36	Laborer
Starky, Frederick	31	Barber
Stephens, Joseph	50	Farmer
Strowd, Noah	40	Porter
Suffiner, Amanda	18	Domestic Servant
Swayen, Harry	60	Laborer
Tanner, Jane	45	Cook & Washer
Taylor, Aaron	55	Laborer
Taylor, Jerry	24	Laborer
Taylor, Liza	45	None

Taylor, Marillo	34	None
Taylor, Mary	65	None
Taylor, William	20	Laborer on RR
Teal, William	58	Farm Laborer
Thomas, Charlotte	35	None
Thomas, John	30	Laborer
Thomas, Joseph	12	None
Thompson, Harry	72	Laborer
Thompson, Henry	39	Farm Laborer
Thompson, Jack	18	None
Thompson, Oma	30	Distillery Worker
Thurman, Andrew	35	Farm Laborer
Thurman, Harriett	35	Keeping House
Tillman, George	42	Farm Laborer
Tillman, Joseph	18	Farm Laborer
Trigg, Moses	37	Blacksmith
Turner, Amie	19	None
Turner, Fannie	12	Domestic Servant
Turner, Lettie	92	None
Turner, Roena	23	Keeping House
Vance, Isban	72	Domestic Servant
Vannoy, Clarissa	40	Keeping House
Vanoy, Nancy	18	Cook
Wagner, Andrew	28	Laborer on RR
Wagner, Nedd	52	Laborer
Wagoner, Lucy	18	None
Wait, Anderson	14	None
Waite, Hyatt	50	Farm Laborer
Walker, Henry	24	Farm Laborer
Ward, Adaline	18	Domestic Servant

Waterson, John	55	Blacksmith
Whitaker, Robert	34	Farming
White, Fanny	15	None
White, Jacob	20	Sawmill Worker
Wilborn, Robert	25	Farm Laborer
Wilkerson, George	11	Laborer
Wilkerson, Jim	15	None
Wilkerson, Joseph	41	Laborer
Wilkinson, Nancy	40	None
Wilkinson, Tom	50	Laborer
Williams, Bud	24	Laborer
Williams, Nancy	40	Domestic Servant
Williams, Nelson	34	Laborer
Willis, Peter	60	Laborer
Willis, Violett	43	Keeping House
Wilson, Harrison	27	Laborer
Wilson, Mary	16	Cook at Shanty
Wilson, Mary	44	Cook
Winton, Agnes	78	Keeping House
Winton, Allen	26	Laborer
Winton, Angeline	18	Cook & Washer
Winton, C.	47	Farm Laborer
Winton, Carroll	30	Shoe Maker
Winton, Charles	40	Farm Laborer
Winton, Francis	20	House Servant
Winton, Francis	21	Domestic Servant
Winton, George	21	Laborer
Winton, Isaac	24	None
Winton, Jackson	50	Laborer
Winton, Judia	46	House Servant

Winton, Mary	35	House Servant	
Winton, Matt	24	Laborer	
Winton, Philip	55	None	
Wooten, Abram	53	Farm Laborer	
Wooten, Hettie	18	None	
Wooton, Lucy	21	None	
Young, Tandie	56	Farm Laborer	

Blacks & Mulattos listed in the 1880 Census:

Below, listed by Districts, are the Negroes and Mulattos living in Coffee County, their ages and their occupations. Just the heads of household are listed and the number of people in that home given. Children who are listed were living in a white household.

District 1	Age	Occupation	Number in Household Race Black	Race Mulatto
Thomas, James	20	Work on Farm	1	
Ashley, Mack	50	Farmer	16	
Wood, Henry	48	Laborer	11	
Blair, Milley	65	House	5	
Brown, Simeon	64	Shoe maker	3	
Estes, Dock	35	Laborer	4	
Ashley, Jennie	19	Servant	1	
Williams, Alf	24	Laborer	3	
Sutton, Eliza	26	Servant	4	
Blair, James	2		1	
Jacales, James	33	Farm Labor	10	

Lyons, Greenville	35	Black Smith	8	
Keele, Harriet	16	Servant	1	
Hickerson, Joe	21	Laborer	2	

District 2

Cortner, Alice	18	Domestic Ser	1	
Rayburn, Oten	19	Farm Laborer	3	
Jernigan, Adam	35	Farm Laborer	7	
Curlee, Oma	62	Domestic Ser	2	
Short, Jefferson	41	Farm Laborer	7	
Hall, William	54	Farm Laborer	2	1
Avery, Samuel	26	Farm Laborer	7	
Jacobs, David	43	Farm Laborer	7	
Robinson, Martin	56		6	
Watterson, John	70	Black Smith	5	
Patton, Andy	70	Farm Laborer	4	1
Scott, Hulda	57	Farm Laborer	10	
Johnson, Jerry	43	Farm Laborer	3	
Miller, Richard	30	Farm Laborer	3	1
Osborn, Barkly	38		6	
Ashly, Milas	56	Stone Mason	7	
Walker, Harry	29	Farmer	8	
Keele, Thomas	56	Farmer	6	
Ramsey, Peter	55	Farm Laborer	14	
Norton, Moriah	55	Keep House	3	
Pinkard, David	19	Laborer	1	
Finney, John	60	Carpenter	9	
Bailey, Henry	10	Servant	1	
Hunt, Isham	28	Laborer	5	
Cotner, Vina	45	Domestic Servant	2	

Davis, William	35	Laborer	8	
Norville, Cisero	14	Servant	2	
George, Maxwell	32	Work on Farm	5	
Dillard. Sarah	26	Domestic Servant	2	
Ashly, Samuel	25	Laborer	1	
Owens, Ab	50	Farm Laborer	2	
Carden, Angeline	34	Keep House	5	
Rayburn, Lewis	25	Farm Laborer	3	
Ashly, Edney	17	Servant	1	
Hickerson, Ann	25	Servant	1	
Teal, Harry	7	Servant	1	
Cotner, Sallie	30	Servant	3	
Neal, James	28	Laborer	3	

District 3

Alley, Jack	81	Farmer	1	1
Jacobs, Norris	3		2	
Brown, Abrams	52	Farmer	1	2
Moppins, Abner	78	Farmer	3	1
Scruggs, Morris	33	Rock Mason	2	1
Davis, Eden	16		2	
Lane, David	55	Farmer	3	
Davis, John	13	Servant	1	
Canon, Alice	15	Boarder	1	
Hoard, Henry	15	Laborer	1	
Powers, Charles	34	Farmer	5	
Farrar, Tenes	70	Boarder		1
Jacobs, Harry	28	Black Smith	2	
Arnold, Albert	24	Laborer	6	
Powers, Moses	52	Farmer	3	2

Name	Age	Occupation		
Armstrong, Isham	58	Laborer	5	1
Austell, Clarisa	30	Keep House	3	
Harris, Henry	52	Farmer		8
Ward, Benjamin	51	Farmer		7
Scruggs, Pleasant	55	Black Smith	4	
Bailey, Julia	66		4	
Carney, George	53	Farmer	4	
Farrar, Willis	29	Farmer	3	1
Scruggs, Wash.	32	Farmer	6	1
Burns, Albert	42	Farmer	6	
Easly, Jeff	37	Farmer	3	
Alley, Henry	32	Laborer	2	
McMichael, T	65	Keep House	4	
Carren, Gaven	60	Laborer	8	
McGill, Cora	6		2	
McGill, Benjamin	23	Laborer	6	
McGill, Andy	19	Laborer	2	
Tillinan, Joseph	27	Laborer	3	
Davidson, Jane	53	Servant		1
Teal, Martha	35	Keep House	6	
Robertson, James E.	8	Servant		1
Scott, Mary	17	Servant	1	
Moppins, Grun	30	Farmer	2	1
Pinkard, James	25	Farmer	2	
Mason, Ailry	50	Keep House	1	
Robertson, Ann	40	Keep House		8
Mason, Ephraim	33	Farmer	9	
Hamilton, Elijah	29	Farmer	6	
Patton, Henry	36	Laborer	7	
Lane, Mattie	15	Servant	1	

Hickerson, Spencer	82	Laborer	2	
Jernett, John	33	Laborer	6	
Maxfield, Chas.	52	Carpenter		9
Teal, William	56	Farmer	6	
Norvill, Pharoh	45	Laborer		3
Miller, Richard	25	School Teacher	1	3
Jakes, Booker	81	Farmer	2	
Lackey, John	74	Laborer	2	1
Keele, George	45	Laborer	10	
Bounds, Wesley	38	Laborer	1	2
McGill, Henry	53	Farmer	5	1
Smith, James	46	Farmer		14

District 4 and 17

District 5

District 5 and 17

Hale, Houston	19	Laborer	1	
Hale, Luke	21	Laborer	1	
Jenkins, Jessie	20	Farmer	1	
Elliot, Jefferson	21	Farm Laborer	1	

District 6

Kincannon, Susan	22	Servant	5	
Speace, William	29	Servant	1	
Waggoner, Bettie	14	Servant	1	
Speace, Charley	17	Servant	2	
Winton, Amanda	15	Servant	1	
Taylor, Berry	18	Farm Hand	1	
Smith, Lee	18	Farm Hand	1	
Vannoy, Jane	15	Keep House		6

Name	Age	Occupation		
Black, Alfred	38	Board. Pauper	1	
Roughton, Henry	13	Servant	1	
Foster, Luan	20	Servant	1	
Johnson, Tillman	51	Farmer	10	
Briant, Hannah	15	Servant	1	
Hill, Sarah	22	Servant	1	
Elliott, Henry	14	Servant		1
Rich, Samuel	50	Laborer		9
Rodes, Lavinia	22	Servant		1
Rodes, Lucinda	16	Servant		1
Willis, Aggie	19	Servant	1	
Johnson, Fanny E.	30	Servant	1	
Rodes, Meda	17	Servant	1	
Lane, Luke	28	Laborer	9	
Layne, George	24	Laborer		3
Smartt, Eliza	61	Servant		1
Hill, Susan	57	Servant	1	
Winton, Delilah	42	Servant	1	
Turner, Samuel	38	Laborer		7
Etter, Louisa	24	Servant		1
Kincannon, Belle	24	Servant	1	
Elliott, Mary	33	Servant		1
Wilson, Lucy	45	Keep House	7	
Elliott, Lucinda	55	Keep House	1	
Vannoy, Clarissa	55	Keep House		2
Austill, George	24	Laborer		1
Elliott, Alfred	29	Laborer	4	
Vannoy, Jennie	21	Wash & Iron		5
Holden, David	30	Rheumatism	3	
Brewer, Lindsay	38	Laborer	6	

Winton, Sarah	40	Wash & Iron	4		
Lumpkin, Arthur	42	Barber		3	
Bowman, Rufus	21	Laborer	1		
Blair, Mary	18	Servant	1		

District 7

Sanders, Abram	84	Farmer		2	
Layne. Sheaker	32	Farming	4		
Nevils, Frances	30	Keep House	3		
Layne, John	60	Farming	4		
Rice, Eliza J.	24	Servant	4		
Crawford, McMillian	28	Farmer		6	
Gunn, Druzilla	8	Hired	1		
Henly, Roxena	7	At Home	4		
Jenkins, Eliza	8	Servant	1		
Jenkins, Hannah	16	Servant	3		
Rowe, Robert	52	Black Smith	3		
Rowe, Foster	30	Farming	4		
Rowe, Hardy	25	Farming	4		
McQuiddy, Alice	21	Servant	1		

District 8

Ramsey, Nelson	50	Farming	7		1
Fults, George	17	Hired	1		
Winton, George	33	At Home	1		

District 9

Perkins, Cory	22	Farm Laborer	3		
Roach, Potter	22	Farm Laborer	3		
Brown, Jack	46	Farm Laborer	5		

Hammins, Arington	73	Farming	7	
Gwynn, John	39	Farm Laborer	7	
Winton, Wiliam	22	Farm Laborer	1	
Northcut, William	21	Farm Laborer	1	
Winton, Jack	60	Farm Laborer	7	
Pearson, Maggie	12	Servant	1	
Bryan, Joseph	41	Farming	8	
Lane, Calvin	54	Farming	4	2
Winton, Charls	78	Farm Laborer	4	
MacGee, Benjamin	50	Farm Laborer	7	
Hill, Alexander	45	Farm Laborer	13	
Gross, Joseph	24	Farm Laborer	1	
Jones, Andrew	21	Farm Laborer	1	
Davis, Mary	29	Servant Cook	1	

District 10:

Foster, John	45	Farmer	6
Bowls, Pleasant	64	Farm Laborer	2
Winton, Martin	38	Farm Laborer	8
Hill, Chelsey	38	Farm Laborer	6
Brown, Martha	50	Keep House	7
Turner, Bryan	54	Farm Laborer	2
Lyons, Amand	19	Servant Cook	1
Lyons, Bryan	44	Farm Laborer	8
Hill, Abram	54	Farm Laborer	2
Turner, Henry	45	Farm Laborer	4
Bowen, Frank	72	Farm Laborer	2
Baugh, Willis	40	Work on RR	8
Baugh, Gilbert	36	Work on RR	5
Snell, Ellen	38	Keep House	2

McGill, Pleasant	40	Farm Laborer	10	
Smith, Aaron	52	Farming	3	
Price, Wesley	42	Farm Laborer	7	
Brown, Cloricy	22	Washing	3	
Wooten, Jessie	47	Farming	12	
Wilborn, Robert	28	Farm Laborer	2	
Roads, Charles	54	Black Smith	9	
Logan, John	30	Farming	2	3
Roads, Rebecca	63	Keep House	6	
Foster, John	45	Farming	6	

District 11:

Sheid, Samuel	50	Farming	6	
Austell, Ned	24	Farming	2	
Thomkins, Mary	9	At Home	1	
McGowan, Thomas	16	Hired	1	
Willis, Hence	12	Hired	1	
Henley, William	38	Farming	2	
Rowe, Fayette	22	Farming	9	
McGowan, Eli	22	Farming	3	
Crockett, Orange	51	Farming	10	
Willis, Peter	70	Farming	5	
Gunn, Anderson	19	Hireling	3	
Phillips, Shack	47	Farming	2	1
Crockett, Harry	47	Farming	7	
Crockett, Isaac	64	Farming	2	
Cunningham, Ransom	70	Servant	1	
Stephenson, Jesse	26	Farming	4	
Stephenson, Joseph	24	Farming	6	
Rice, Henry	24	Farming	6	

Rice, Flemming	45	Farming	2	
Nevils, Antny	30	Farming	11	
Nevils, George	25	Farming	8	
Harris, Emily	68	Keep House	8	1
Rutledge, Emma	25	Keep House	3	
Jackson, Jonas	28	Farming	5	
Wooton, Lucy	25	Keep House	6	
Brock, Drusilla	50	Keep House	2	
Bryan, Taylor	25	Farming	5	
Crockett, Martha	26	At Home	5	
Sims, Taylor	26	Hireling	5	
Crockett, James	24	Farming	7	

District 12:

Gilliam, Joseph	28	Farming	3	
Kennely, Ben	35	Hired	3	
Oliver, John	18	Servant	3	
Kennely, Harriet	33	Keep House	4	
Willis, Thomas	18	Hired	1	
Wilkinson, Amanda	18		1	
Wilkinson, Henry	28	Farmer	5	
Bryan, Mary	70	Servant	1	
Clepper, Henry	50	Farming	9	
Hill, George	31	Farming	1	5
Taylor, Jackson	23	Farming	1	4
Taylor, Mariah	40	Keep House		4
Austell, Sarah	45	Keep House	5	
Willis, Violet	45	Keep House	3	
Wilkinson, Joseph	49	Farming	6	
Rowland, Button	22		1	

Wilkinson, Thomas	1	At Home	1
Wooton, John	20	Loafer Got no house	1
Turner, Frank	25	Hired	1
Clark, George	12	Servant	1
Perkins, Frances	56	Servant	1
Austell, Anonymous	20	Hired	1
Willis, Anderson	48	Black Smith	11
Patton, Isaac	51	Farmer	3
Kelly, Martin	40	Farmer	4
Reynolds, John	53	Farmer	10
Burnette, Rena	22		3
Reynolds, Anonymous	77	Farmer	3
Foster, Isaac	17		1
McGowan, Eli	56	Farmer	14
Patton, Mariah	60	Keep House	7
Patton, Mirandy	30	Keep House	1
Patton, Thomas	17	At Home	7
Patton, Victoria	31	Keep House	5
Patton, Harrison	25	Farmer	4
Willis, George	22	Hired	1
Turner, Frank	27	Farmer	3
Farris, Rufus	25	Farmer	9
Patton, Benjamin	56	Farmer	6
Cunningham, Ben	18	Hired	1
Layne, Hannah	80	Keep House	2
Gunn, Jane	50	At Home	3
Winton, Isaac	36	Farmer	2
Vannoia, Lewis	21	Farmer	3
Winton, Creasy	60	Keep House	4
Reynolds. Phillip	55	Black Smith	12

Icher, Beck	24	Farmer	5	
Rutledge, Jimmie	60	Keep House	1	
Wilkerson, Harrison	36	Farmer	6	
Gilliam, Rose	54	Keep House	2	
Clark, Hannah	7	Servant	1	
Thompson, James	25	Farmer	4	
Arnold, John	25	Farmer	2	
Austell, Charlie	55	Farmer	1	

District 13

Thompson, Henry	70	Farmer	6	
Starkie, Frederick	57	Barber	9	
Davidson, Louis	54	Farmer	8	
Touchstone, John	55	Laborer	1	4
Smartt, Andy	39	Laborer	1	4
Smartt, Burnell	65	Laborer	4	
Hampton, Aaron	57	Farmer	9	
Harris, Lettie	32	Keep House	3	
Wileman, Louis	26	Laborer	3	
Robb, Henry	29	Laborer	8	
Patterson, John	25	Labor on RR	4	
Daly, Margaret	18	Servant	2	
Harris, Drunell	12	Servant	1	
Whitmore, Jesica	44	Servant	1	
Crisman, Washington	36	Laborer	5	
Bonner, William	24	Laborer	4	
Bonner, Chas	53	Laborer	3	
Washington, Eliza	15	Servant	2	
Watkins, Robert	61	Meth Preach	4	
Pearson, Henry	40	Engineer H&S		7

Farris, Milley	28	Servant	3	
Jones, Fanny	23	Servant	6	
Berry, Henry	40	Laborer	4	
Smartt, Thos	30	Laborer	4	1
Shafner, Jo	50	Laborer	3	
Hanly, Alf	75	Gardener	2	
Daniels, Rose	26	Keep House	2	
King, Wash	31	Laborer	3	
Smith, Berry	28	Laborer	5	
Havond, Alfred	54	Laborer	3	
Simms, Gideon	22	Laborer	2	
Havond, Sallie	37	Servant	1	
Wagner, Andrew	40	Laborer	6	
Cook, Alex	50	Laborer	8	
Jenkins, Henry	23	Laborer	1	2
Cook, Elizabeth	45	Keep House	6	
Morris, Samuel	22	Works on RR	2	
Harden, Abner	60	Laborer	3	
Cole, Charlotte	50	Chambermaid		1
Whitson, Alex	26	Servant	1	
Snodgrass, Jno.	18	Servant	1	
Cook, Brown	24	Servant	1	
Hatcher, William	30	Servant	1	
Stevens, William	32	Servant	1	
Hester, Ann	35	Servant		1
Shelby, Geo.	21	Servant		1
Reynolds, Speak	24	Work on RR	2	
Nelson, Austen	30	Laborer		3
Petty, Sallie	38	Keep House	3	1
Sherrell, Moses	50	Laborer	7	

Curtis, Rhena	20	Keep House	2	
Petty, Mary	42	Keep House	1	
Stewart, Malinda	27	Laundress		7
Morely, Estell	55	Laborer	7	
Simms. Jo	21	Porter in store		2
Jenkins, Peyton	45	Laborer	3	
Rankin, Douglas	36	Minister	1	3
Newton, Henry	54	Laborer	2	
Waggoner, Sampson	22	Laborer	3	
Reynolds, Speak	27	Laborer on RR		2
Spron, Noah	45	Servant	3	
Jenkins, Andrew	35	Laborer	7	
Oldham, Cherry	64	Keep House	2	2
Hall, Cherry	39	Keep House	2	
Sheron, Elijah	35	Work on RR	5	
Flemming, Jno	38	Work on RR	2	
McGee, Robert	38	RR Laborer	6	
Oldham, George	50	Carpenter	7	
Ross, Rueben	27	Plasterer	1	4
Lock, Richard	26	Laborer	4	
Cole, Henry	27	Laborer	1	1
Becket, Andrew	25	Laborer	4	
Neville, Sallie	25	Keep House	4	
Jenkins, Green	45	Laborer	6	2
Strainler, Saml	30	Laborer	4	
Farris, Thomas	32	Laborer	4	
Whittaker, Jane	42	Laundress	1	
Everett, Isaac	47	Laborer	4	
Kirby, Robert	45	Laborer	3	
Patterson, Thomas	40	Laborer	3	

Rhoton, Kate	30	Keep House	5		
Whittaker, Sterling	36	Farm Hand	7		
Hickerson, Thomas	51	Laborer	4		
Lewis, Frank	48	Laborer	7		
Landers, Jo	34	Wheel & Spoke	2	4	
Nelson, John	25	Laborer		3	
Monroe, Chas.	42	Black Smith	6		
Cook, Henry	23	RR Worker	7		
Williams, Bryant	30	RR Porter	3		
Reagan, Charlotte	60	Laundress	9		
Walden, Sarah	67	Keep House		2	
Webb, Robert	51	Laborer	4		
Beaty, Anthony	54	Laborer	4		
Kennedy, Louis	55	Laborer	3		
Lusk, Henry	40	Laborer	3	3	
Rutledge, Martha	40	Keep House	1	3	
Duff, Phillis	58	Keep House	4	1	
Couch, Wren	23	RR Laborer	5		
Blanton, Thadeus	61	Carpenter	1	2	
Taylor, Eliza	50	Keep House		5	
Hogan, Edward	10	Servant	2		
Boney, Adeline	42	Wash & Iron	1		

District 14

Kincannon, Allen	50	Farm Laborer	4		
Nelson, Mack	19	Farm Laborer	1		
Taylor, Eldy	12	Farm Laborer	1		
Kincannon, Robert	13	Farm Laborer	1		
Taylor, Luke	35	Farm Laborer	5	1	
Kincannon, Emily	33	Servant	2		

Name	Age	Occupation		
Nelson, Harriett	38	Keep House	4	
Taylor, Claeborne	25	Farm Laborer	4	
Hale, Andy	70	Farmer	6	
Hale, Solomon	30	Farmer	5	
Taylor, Iore	35	Farmer	7	
Kincannon, Chaney	22	Keep House	2	

District 15

Name	Age	Occupation		
Rice, James	21	Laborer	1	
Cunningham, Robert	33	Farm Laborer	9	
Cunningham, Neal	75	Farm Laborer	8	
Gwyn, Thomas	30	Farm Laborer	6	
Davis, Madison	65	Farmer	2	
Edwards, Vincent	105		1	
Ramsey, Willis	47	Farmer	6	
Cunningham, Edi	67	Farmer	2	
King, Hanah	68	Servant	1	1

District 17

Name	Age	Occupation		
Hart, William	16	Farm Laborer		1
Davidson, Wisley	57	Work on RR	8	
Bowman, Thomas	28	Work on RR	6	
Savage, Dallas	27	Work on RR	4	
Gaunt, Steven	61	Farmer	3	
Hickerson, James	26	Farmer	1	4
Hawkins, Clarissa	29	Servant	1	
Ray, Robert	20	Laborer	1	
Hickerson, Nancy	20	Keep House	5	1
Hickerson, Henry	51	Farmer	9	
Pepper, Henry	25	Farm Laborer	2	

Davidson, Henry	16	Farm Laborer	1	
Smith, Jery	23	Farmer	1	1
Couch, Samuel	35	Farmer	5	
Osborne, Joseph	18	Farmer	1	
Serigg, William	20	Farm Laborer	1	

The 1880 Census of Coffee County showed 1,475 Black and 220 Mulatto individuals for a total of 1,695. Farming and Laborers were the most common occupations.

I got shoes, you got shoes
All o' God's chillun got shoes
When I get to heab'n I'm goin' to put on my shoes
I'm goin' to walk all ovah God's Heab'n
Heab'n , Heab'n
Ev'rybody talkin' 'bout heab'n ain't goin' dere
Heab'n, Heab'n
I'm goin' to walk all ovah God's Heab'n

COFFEE COUNTY, TN, AREA LYNCHINGS

By Jess Lewis, Coffee County Historian
(Reprinted from the Coffee County Historical Quarterly, Vol. 28, #1 & 2)

Caution... The following article contains information concerning extreme acts of violence that occurred in our area, in a darkened time of the past. Some may consider it distasteful. It perhaps should not be read by the faint of heart or by our younger readers.

Lynching is a subject that many people, especially in the South, are uncomfortable with. Nevertheless, it is a part of our history. Most people think of hanging and racial violence when lynching is mentioned, but that is not necessarily true. Webster defines lynching simply as "putting a person to death by mob action without due process of law." It often included torture, burning at a stake (or otherwise), castration, disfigurement and dismemberment while still alive. Parts of the victim's body, as well as pieces of clothing, were often kept as souvenirs. Often, large groups including men, women and children took part in this barbaric activity. Pictures and postcards were sometimes made at the scene and were freely circulated and even mailed. The images included not only the victims, but faces in the crowd as well. In general, especially in earlier times, the legal authorities seemed to look the other way at times, or sometimes even participated themselves. Even when brought before courts, many were charged only with manslaughter, or simply with carrying a pistol. Extradition between states was just about unheard of, so simply escaping across the state line permanent or at least until the "heat was off" often times ended the entire matter.

Often, the lynch victims were, in fact, guilty of capital crimes. Some had confessed, some were tried and found guilty, while others had eyewitnesses to their crimes. But often they were not guilty, or were guilty of some lesser crime. Occasionally, family or friends were killed at the same time, to "get rid of the witnesses." People who aided prospective lynch victims in escaping were sometimes killed in fits of rage. At any rate, these people were denied due process under the laws of our country.

During the history of the United States, more white people have been lynched than any other group. This includes robbers, thieves, gunmen, murderers and competing "foreigners" in the Old West. In fact, every state in the continental United States with the exception of Massachusetts, Rhode Island, New Hampshire and Vermont has had lynching casualties. But in the Old South, during the post-Civil War era, many more black people were lynched than any other group.

Coffee County, Tennessee has had its share, along with surrounding counties. Between 1890 and 1936, there have been at least six documented lynchings in Coffee County.

On August 25, 1891, William Lewis, a black man, previously charged with burglary, was lynched in Tullahoma, TN. The reason was" being drunk and saucy to white folks." No record has been found where anyone was ever charged with this crime.

On May 17, 1892, Charles Everett was charged with housebreaking at the home of A. Y. Smith in Tullahoma and the attempted rape of a white woman. He pled guilty to the housebreaking, but not guilty to the rape charge. He was lynched in Manchester, Tennessee, on May 19, 1892.

On October 14, 1895, Eugene Vannoy, a black man, was lynched in Manchester, TN, for "keeping a white woman." Six men, some being from local prominent families, were indicted in January, 1896, for "unlawfully and feloniously by night time while in mask and disguise and while prowling, traveling, riding and walking through the country in Coffee County, Tennessee to the disturbance of the peace, assault one Eugene Vannoy with pistols, guns, sticks, with large whips, switches and other dangerous and deadly weapons." They were due to appear in court, but during the next court session, on May 25, 1896, none of the above could be found in the area. One, at least, was known to have left the area for Texas, never to return. The case was moved to the retired docket, with the understanding that it would be renewed if the defendants were ever found "in the jurisdiction of this court."

On March 8, 1905, Rance Gwynn, a black man, was removed from "the calaboose" in Tullahoma, by "parties unknown" and hung on a nearby tree. Gwinn had previously been charged with larceny, but had served his time and returned to the area, where he was soon again arrested for larceny and suspicion of arson. A great uproar occurred in Tullahoma and the surrounding area, over the lynching outrage. Editorials were run in both of the local newspapers condemning this act and town meetings were held to raise a reward to find the parties. No record has been found where anyone was ever charged.

On February 10, 1918, Jim McIlherron, a black man of Estill Springs, Tennessee, was about to be drafted into the Army. According to later gossip and testimony, he decided that before he left, he would "Shoot up the town." Two men were killed and another was fatally wounded. The town was outraged. A mob soon suspected a black minister, G. W. Nich, of Prairie Plains of aiding the man to escape town. His house was surrounded by a heavily armed posse, and gunfire soon followed. The record shows that Rev. Nich was shot while resisting arrest. Shortly afterwards, McIlherron was located in Warren County. A heavily armed posse of 27 men passed through Manchester and Morrison on the train, with Smartt Station being their destination. McIlherron was found and surrounded in a barn, on the Collins River, about 4 miles from McMinnville, where he had taken refuge, the previous night. The posse, now 75 to 100 men, opened fire and McIlherron returned fire with his two pistols. Finally, wounded and out of ammunition, he was captured. He was returned to Estill Springs, where he was burned at a stake, by the infuriated people.

On June 23, 1934, the Patton Chapel (Negro) Church near Prairie Plains, in Coffee County, was having an "Ice Cream Festival." Eight white men decided to crash the party and trouble soon started. During a shoving match, one of the white men was hit over the head by a church deacon, Dick Lou Wilkerson. Mr. Wilkerson was a well-liked and respected man in the community, by both black and white neighbors. Sensing more trouble, Wilkerson ran from the church. The white men then armed themselves, and stealing Wilkerson's car, ran up and down the roads, trying to find him. They broke into his home and ransacked the place, and his wife ran into hiding. Finally, in the early hours of the morning they found him along the road. They fired and wounded him with a shotgun, but he jumped the fence, into an oat field. They followed and fired many shotgun and pistol shots into his body. The eight men were arrested, tried and found guilty of manslaughter in the Coffee County Circuit Court, on September 6, 1934. Three men were sentenced to 5 years in prison and the other five were sentenced to 2 years each. Mr. Wilkerson is buried in the Tate Cemetery, along the Betsy Willis to Prairie Plains Road, in an unmarked grave.

Other known lynchings in nearby Counties. (Some of these have not been fully researched...):

York Douglas lynched in McMinnville, Tennessee, April 17, 1896.

Henry Noles lynched Winchester, Tennessee, April 25, 1901.

Walter Grer lynched Shelbyville, Tennessee, February 19, 1912.

David Neal lynched Shelbyville, Tennessee, February 19, 1912.

Green Boman lynched Shelbyville, Tennessee, February 19, 1912.

Thomas Lillard was lynched for rape in Woodbury, Tennessee, on June 28, 1892.

William Chambers lynched Bell Buckle, Tennessee, August 11, 1899.

Mary Motlow, Sam Motlow, Ned Waggoner, and Will Waggoner, all black people, lynched in Moore County, Tennessee, on November 4, 1893, for "Barn Burning."

A Lynching at Tullahoma
(from The Manchester Times, March 8, 1905)

Tullahoma Press, March 8 – Rance Gwynn, a colored man about 22 years old, was taken from the calaboose here this morning between 1 and 2 o'clock by unknown parties and hanged. Gwynn was arrested by Deputy Sheriff John F. Dwyer on Tuesday afternoon on a warrant charging larceny. The preliminary trial was to have been held before Squire W. J. Davidson this morning at 8 o'clock.

Officer Dwyer stated that he was at the calaboose about 12 o'clock and everything was all right with Gwynn up to that hour. There had been no excitement concerning the arrest, and the hanging of the negro was a shock and complete surprise to everyone here.

Gwynn was taken from the calaboose and carried about fifty yards to the rear of the prison to a tree, where he was strung up. The rope used was no larger than a window cord, and the limb to which he was suspended was not more than two inches in diameter.

When discovered the body had no clothing on except a shirt and pair of socks.

Gwynn had been in the penitentiary for larceny and had only been out a short time. He was arrested yesterday afternoon, charged with stealing about $40 from R. E. Day. Gwynn was also suspected of having set fire to Mr. Day's house in order to conceal the theft.

The people of Tullahoma are very much mortified over the affair. There is no excitement, and a thorough investigation will be made.

[A calaboose: slang for jail or prison]

FREE BLACKS YEARS LATER

Freed slaves moved on with their lives. Most handled their newfound freedom well; some had problems adjusting; some established homes and families; surely, all experienced the joys and sorrows that are a part of everyday life. And, decades later the word "slave" was surfacing again – often, but not always, in obituaries.

In August of 1915 the Manchester Times gave a report on "Old Uncle Ned," who had passed the Century Mark. Living in Owensboro, KY at that time, Ned Irvin had reached the age of 110. The article continued, "Ned dates back to 1805 when he was born at New Manchester, TN. He was the son of a slave and that way fell into the hands of slave owners. At his birth, Ned belonged to Massah (sic) John Hickerson of New Manchester, who was a rich slave owner with a large plantation in TN. For his childhood he was known as Ned Hickerson. At age 20 he was sold to William Little. He was swapped more than a dozen times and was called in many cases by the name of his many masters. All the white people living during Uncle Ned's younger years have passed away and there are no persons now living that were born before he reached the age of 50, that he remembers."

In May 1922 the Times was again reporting on Uncle Ned. This time it was his obituary. At 118 years of age, the old Negro had died at his home in Owensboro, KY. The paper reported that a few years previously Uncle Ned had "visited the Manchester Fair, where he was one of the main attractions." In his younger years he had worked on the railroads in Virginia under John Quincy Adams and had helped build the L. and N. railroad into Owensboro. He was survived by three sons, Ed, Charlie and Bert (Berl).

The little ditty that was included in Uncle Ned Irvin's obituary in May of 1922:

"Lay down the shovel and the hoe,

Take up the fiddle and the bow,

There's no more work for ole Uncle Ned,

He's gone where the good n_____ go."

In July 1938 the Times carried the obituary of Howard Elam. At 93 years of age, Howard had died at his home at Smith's Chapel. He had been "a slave before the Civil War, belonging to James Elam of Fosterville, the grandfather of Mrs. E. P. Vaughan of Manchester. Mr. Elam advised the Negro, after giving him his freedom and a sum of money, to come to Coffee County and buy land for a home. This he did, buying and building on a tract near Smith's Chapel, where his house and barns were patterned after those of Mr. Elam at Fosterville."

Howard left behind his 3 daughters and 5 sons: Ida Hill, Lou Hickerson, Jane Bonner, Walter, Will, James, Glen and Tom Elam.

The following story ran in the Manchester Times on Friday, October 18, 1895. It details the story of the killing of Eugene Vannoy by a group of men on Monday, October 14, 1895.

KILLED BY A MOB

A Crowd attempted to whip Eugene Vannoy, when he unmasked and exposed several of them, and was shot to death.

Two of the mob accidentally shot by their companions – The killing is unanimously condemned by good citizens.

Early Monday night, sometime half past 8-o'clock, a crowd of men went to the home of Eugene Vannoy, colored, and called him up, telling him they wanted him to go 'possom hunting. It being a common thing for some of his friends to come by for him to join in such sport, he at once got out of bed and prepared to accompany them. As soon as he emerged from the door of the kitchen, in which he slept, he was seized by two or more men, who carried him off toward the field gate near the house. As soon as he discovered that he was in the hands of those not his friends he began calling to R. M. Vannoy, who was in the residence to which the kitchen belonged, telling him they were going to whip him. By this time Mr. Vannoy had reached the yard, when he was taken in charge by two men, who prevented him from going to where Eugene was. He pleaded with them not to hurt Eugene, saying if he had done anything wrong, he (Vannoy) would see to it he was punished for it. In the meantime, those having the negro had gotten him about forty yards from the house, he struggling with all his might to get free, and shouting that they were going to whip him. Mr. Vannoy asked him who it was, and he answered, giving the name of a person well known here. This reply evidently sealed his doom, as at once he exclaimed "_ _ has killed me," calling the name of a citizen of this town. Several shots were fired in rapid succession at this time, and though wounded to death, he managed to escape from them having him in charge (due it is supposed to the fact that two of the party were accidently shot by their comrades), and ran back toward the house, nearly reaching it before he fell. He died a few minutes later. It is supposed that the mob intended to whip him, as a lot of switches were found on the ground there the next morning, but in the scuffle, he tore off the masks and recognized a number of his assailants, and then it was prosecution for them or death to the negro, and they had the weapons.

The crime charged against Eugene Vannoy was criminal intimacy with a white girl living near-by, aged 14 years last Tuesday. The mother and step-father of the child were seen by the writer on Tuesday and questioned closely as to the relations between their daughter and Eugene, both unhesitatingly answered that they had never seen anything the least improper in their actions. The child has up to a recent date had to carry what water the family used from the Vannoy spring, passing the house, and consequently seeing Eugene daily, and like all other children would have done, she would stop and talk with him in the yard. They said he would frequently come to their house at night with his guitar and play till bedtime, but that at no time did anything occur in the actions of either he or the girl which could possibly be construed as to infer intimacy existed between them. In reply to a question, the step-father stated that only once had the girl gone out of the house at night while Eugene was there, and remained out until he was gone, and that on this occasion she remained on the outside five or ten minutes, and that her mother scolded her for it asking her where she had been. Asked as to a report that he had been told by a neighbor a few weeks ago that it was being circulated that Eugene and his step-daughter were criminally intimate, and that the fact could be proven by Gib Perry, he said that he had been so informed, and that upon hearing he went to Perry about it, and that he (Perry) denied positively having made any such statement. In short, neither parent believed the negro guilty of improper conduct with their daughter.

The little girl was interviewed by a representative of the TIMES Tuesday, and denied emphatically that Eugene had never addressed her improperly or attempted in any manner to take liberties with her person; that never had he accompanied her to the spring but once, and then she was accompanied by an 8-year old sister; that she was never in the Vannoy house alone with deceased, and that she was never alone with him anywhere. In regard to the report that she was in a delicate condition, another denial was made with the girl expressing a willingness to submit to an examination by physicians to not only prove she was telling the truth, but to further establish the fact that she had never been criminally intimate with Vannoy or any other man.

The foregoing are the facts as near as the TIMES could gather from those supposed to be familiar with them. To correct a few impressions which have gone out through Nashville papers, we desire to say that the girl is not half-witted, but is one of the brightest children in this entire section; the mob was not composed "of thirty or forty of the best citizens of Manchester and the vicinity," and that the act instead of being considered right by the people of Manchester, is looked upon as the most dastardly and unprovoked murder ever occurred in this vicinity.

The following partial article was printed in the January 31, 1896 Manchester Times and also provides information on the Vannoy murder case:

MOBSTERS INDICTED

The grand jury spent considerable time during the past week investigating the killing of Eugene Vannoy by a mob in October of last year, and it is pretty generally understood a number of indictments have been found against parties supposed to have participated in the killing. Fully a dozen citizens of the town have disappeared since the first of January ...

Judge Smallman authorized the Attorney General to be the prosecutor on the indictments in the Eugene Vannoy murder case.

Vannoy Recalls Days of Slavery

Reprinted from the Manchester Times, Friday Morning, July 7, 1944

"I, Louis Vannoy, am having this printed to let everybody know who I am. I am free-born and am past foure-score (sic) and ten years of age. I was born in the Indian Territory. My mother, Claricy Vannoy, was a full-blooded Cherokee Indian. She and her four children, Jim, Nan, Jennie and Louis were visiting relatives in St. Louis, Mo. when the line was drawn dividing the slave territory from the free. She and her children happened to be on the slave side. I remember the Indian chief making a dash to pull her on the free side, but he was forced back. She and her four children were put on the auction block and sold to Ole Jim Pratt, our first master. He sold us to a man named Hays, who put us on the boat and sent

Clarissa Vannoy
Picture provided by Lorene Hickerson
McReynolds

us to Nashville. Again, we were put on the block and sold to Brisco Vannoy. We stayed in Nashville a long time. Then he bought a farm at Manchester for his son, Lawyer Vannoy and he gave my mother, Claricy and us four children to him to do all his work on the farm.

Manchester, then was a small village, all over trees. You could not see anywhere, only in the roads.

In all our slave life, our family was kept together, but I saw babies sold away from their mother's breast, all their children scattered. I heard the mothers scream about never going to see their children again in this world.

My mother was never whipped like the Negroes. She was an Indian and would not stand for it and they were afraid to whip her. But we children were sometimes whipped, but not so bad. I've seen masters whip their slaves – strop them across a barrel and give them fifty licks on their bare back, dip the strop in salt water and whip the blood out.

Some old masters and mistresses would not let their slaves pray or sing. We did not know what a church was. If we prayed to God we had to turn a washpot down and get around it so we could not be heard praying. If they heard you, you got 50 licks across the barrel.

After we come here we've been here ever since and my mother birthed seven more children – Lawyer Vannoy's children: Laura, Emma, Jane Ella, Will, John, Charlie, Eugene. I have spent many a sad day here and many a good day. I do not know what year I was born, but I know my birthday is August 11. I have worked for some good white men here and I love them. I am a Christian man, a member of the Methodist Church, not so well, just able to go, so pray for me and come to see me my white friends."

LOUIS VANNOY, SR.

~~~~~~

Death comes to Centenarian

Reprinted from the Manchester Times, March 9, 1945

Lewis Vannoy, colored, died at his home here Sunday, March 4th after a brief illness and was buried Wednesday afternoon after funeral services at the Methodist Church of which he had long been a member. The services were held by Rev. Gordon and pallbearers were Clarence Noble, Porter Price, Luther Ashley, Jack Webb, George Tubbs and Bebe Nevills.

Of Indian descent, he with his mother, came from Missouri to Tennessee in the days of slavery, and came by the name of Vannoy, from his last master, Lawyer Vannoy of Manchester. From childhood memories of historical facts, he estimated that he was over 100 years old.

His daughter, Josephine V. Donelson, of Jasper, kept house for him after he became too feeble to be left alone and attended his bedside during his last illness. She accompanied him about two weeks ago on a visit to his daughter, Clara McKinley, who lives on a farm in Warren County.

Many relatives and friends of adjoining counties attended his funeral. Among them were Velmar Wakefield of Chattanooga, a nephew, William Elliott of Nashville, Ruby Buchanan of Tullahoma, his daughter, Clara, of McMinnville, nephew and niece, Colia and Ludie Streeter of Wartrace.

His son, Lewis E. Vannoy of Rockford, Ill was unable to attend the funeral, but will be here next week for a short stay.

He is survived by two brothers, Charley Vannoy of Missouri and Will Vannoy of Kansas, and two sisters, Ella Lee of Humboldt and Laura Holder of Detroit, Mich.

Horace Osborne, 90, Spends Lifetime on Cold Ridge

by Latham Davis

[Reprinted from the Manchester Times, Thursday Morning, July 8, 1976]

"It's spelled c-o-l-d. It's cold up here."

And Horace Osborne ought to know. He's lived on Cold Ridge 90 years, was born about 30 paces from his front step where his garden is now, where the corn was already over his head.

Map-makers and history buffs have disagreed for a long time over the spelling –

some saying it's Cole Ridge, after a man, and some say Coal Ridge.

But Mr. Osborne knows nothing about Mr. Cole. His mammy and pappy were there awhile before he was born.

They're buried down on an old section of Cold Ridge Road that's paved in weeds and dirt in the colored cemetery and he's going to be buried there, too, although the Highway Commission won't keep up the road.

Cold Ridge is in the high ground above Noah, and the gravel and tarred road runs north (after a fashion) to Hoo-Doo, except for the old section that slides off the Ridge to the Murfreesboro Highway.

Mr. Osborne said he

Older Resident – Horace Osborne enjoys the summer sun on the front step of his home on Cole Ridge, where he has lived all his life.
  --Photo by Lathem Davis

remembers when it took half a day to drive a team of mules off Cold Ridge down to Beech Grove each Saturday to get supplies.

Hoodoo, which is nearer, once had three stores, but they did not have the selection Beech Grove stores had, he said.

In his younger days, Mr. Osborne used to walk to work in Beech Grove and make the trip straight off the ridge, in an hour and a half. Cold Ridge Road wasn't traveled much, and even today, Mr. Osborne has to get his mail from a box on McBride's Branch.

He's farmed most of his life and he and his son, who lives down the road, still keep some cattle on several acres that straddle the ridge.

Mr. Osborne now also owns a spring down the hill a ways that he says is the best water you can find, perfect for making whiskey. But if he ever made any, he wouldn't say.

This summer he's busy, even at 90, building a fence, hauling the wooden posts up the road without the aid of a team and digging the holes by hand.

In the days when all the able-bodied men had to spend five days a year on the county roads, Mr. Osborne was overseer on Cold Ridge Road, getting out the labor and keeping the tools.

"I've got to where I can't hardly get around," he said. Maybe not like he once did. But Mr. Osborne still puts in his labor of love on Cold Ridge.

Kids had Fun, Regardless of Race

Memories by Vergil "Hap" Saine

[Reprinted from the Manchester Times, Editorial Section, probably in the late 1980s]

During the 1930s, the African-American neighborhood bordered the Manchester Elementary school yard. Their school was nearby. Mr. Heard Lowry was principal of both schools.

The high school football "park" was between our neighborhood and theirs. It was wiped out when the present Route 55 to McMinnville was constructed.

This park and the school yards with the basketball court were favorite playgrounds for both neighborhoods. Youngsters of pre-high school age, say about 10 to 14, played together without regard to race in those days.

Let me introduce one of my friends of that period.

Shortly after moving back to Manchester in 1980, I was helping my son Jerry sell tires at the former Goodyear store. After making a sale to an African-American gentleman, he gave me his name for the sales ticket as Alonzo Walker. Taken aback, I said, "You mean you're Alonzo Walker? Do you remember a kid named Happy Saine?" He then exclaimed, "You mean you're Happy Saine?" We then hugged each other.

Alonzo was one of several African-American kids who joined me, M. P. Jernigan, T. H. Moore and other local white kids to enjoy playing football and baseball at the old "park." We generally knew each other only by first name. Others included Nathan, Brett, Sugarman, Soap and Wap. We seldom had games one race against the other. We chose sides to even the competition depending on who was present that day.

Alonzo attended high school at the old Davidson Academy in Tullahoma. He was a star back-field man on their football team. He was alderman on the Manchester board during the early 1980s. I remember so well that he supported the Industrial Board in obtaining approval for Manchester to provide water and sewage services for the Interstate Industrial Park being developed at that time.

Our African-American community celebrated August 4 as their "Independence Day" as we whites did July 4. They always featured a baseball game with a team from a nearby town that attracted many white spectators. They had some outstanding players who may have competed for positions in organized baseball had they been given the chance.

Let me mention a few whom I remember clearly. First on my list is "Bee" Webb, catcher, left handed hitter, who lifted many fly balls over the right field fence into Uncle As Brown's garden. His brother, George Webb, was one of their best pitchers, right handed hitter, who slammed balls all the way to the Route 41 highway. Then there was Sherman Lane, a fastball pitcher, and Elsie B. Tubbs, who could handle any position. And another name that most people remember was "Bill" Hill, who lived a long productive life and passed away only a few years ago. He was the fastest runner on the team.

Speaking of the Webb brothers, I must introduce their mother, Frances, and sister, Elizabeth, who lived close by on the property that is now part of the schoolyard. Frances is the one person my mother depended on for assistance on many laundry wash days and for housecleaning, after her daughters had left the nest. Frances also helped with cooking when a larger than normal group of family visitors had to be served. It amazed me how she could step right in and do the cooking for most any dish, just like my mom.

Let me name some other African-Americans who come to mind. "Red" Elliot lived up the Hillsboro Road just beyond the park. He worked for the railroad, and walked by our home early each morning to catch the train as it passed through town on its way to Sparta. "Clab" Lane was an expert for handling the cooking and associated services for big picnics and parties. He was in great demand from various clubs. Finally, the Vannoy family deserves thanks from many in the white community for their masonry services as Manchester developed during those years. My dad reminded me at an early age that Roy Vannoy and his father built the two brick fireplaces and chimney for our home.

Interesting Photo

This photo was found among papers at the Coffee County Historical Society. It depicts a horse harnessed to a wagon or buggy in front of a building with a porch. In the background is a fenced pasture where horses are grazing. An inscription on the back reads W. Anderson and Wes Felton (Negro). This photo was probably staged since the men's stances seem a little too relaxed and there (conveniently) just happened to be someone with a camera on site.

The Vannoy-Hickerson Family Reunion Celebrates 80-plus Years

[Reprinted from the Manchester Times, Wednesday, August 22, 2018]
Press Release

For over 80 years the Vannoy-Hickerson family reunion has been held in Manchester every August. This year the family reunion was held the first weekend of August with approximately one hundred members.

Included in the group was the son of a navigator with the U. S. Army Air Force World War II famous Tuskegee Airmen. He brought his father's Congressional

Members of the Vannoy-Hickerson reunion included visitors from Kansas, Michigan, Nevada, Georgia, New York, New Jersey, Pennsylvania, Virginia and Texas.

Medal of Honor for show and tell. The Congressional Gold Medal is the highest civilian award presented by the U. S. Congress. It is presented to an individual or group for an outstanding deed or act of service to the security, prosperity, and national interest of the United States. This medal was presented to the Tuskegee Airman, African American pilots flying for the U. S. Army Air Forces during World War II. The medal also includes other Tuskegee Airmen such as bombardiers, navigators, mechanics, and other military or civilian men and women who performed ground support duties.

Other relatives in attendance were the parents of a 2016 United States Olympian. Their daughter was a member of the U. S. Track and Field Team during the 2016 Olympics in Rio de Janeiro, Brazil.

Local resident, Joni McReynolds, President of the Tennessee State University Alumni Association, was one of the event planners for the weekend activities.

Activities for the two-day reunion were held at the Coffee County Veterans Building and the Manchester-Coffee County Conference Center.

Some African-American Family Surnames Common to Coffee County

Adams Family	Maxwell Family
Arnold Family	McReynolds Family
Battles Family	Murray Family
Baugh Family	Nevels Family
Biles Family	Northcutt Family
Crutchfield Family	Ramsey Family
Dillard Family	Robinsin Family
Eppinger Family	Sotherland Family
Estill Family	Starks Family
Guest Family	Thomas Family
Hickerson Family	Turner Family
Jackson Family	Wakefield Family
Johnson Family	Walker Family
Little Family	Whitaker Family
Lorance Family	Vannoy Family

Four Brief Family Genealogies

(Info taken from submissions made to the Coffee County Heritage book)

The Elam Family

1. Howard Elam, a slave of James Elam, married Harriet Johnson. Their children were:

    2. Annie Bell Elam

    2. Ida Elam Hill

    2. Tom Elam

    2. Brewer Elam

    2. James Herschell Elam

    2. Jane Elam Bonner

    2. Eddie Elam

    2. Joshua Elam

    2. Walter Elam

   +2. Glenn Lee Elam

    2. Lula Elam Hickerson

    2. Will Jim Elam

+2. Glenn Lee Elam married Gladys Willis Baugh (daughter of Willis and Georgia Scrubbs Baugh) and they had nine children – all born in Coffee County. They were:

    +3. Hershall Lee Elam

    +3. Ernest Walter Elam

    +3. Willie George Elam

    +3. Calvin Franklin Elam

    +3. Clara Mai Elam

    +3. Mary Christine Elam

    +3. Freddie Glenn Elam

    +3. Jessie Ruth Elam

+3. Paul Howard Elam

+3. Herschell Lee Elam married Sarah J. Thomas and they had no children.

+3. Ernest Walter Elam married (1) Ida Mai Lee and they had nine children:

    4. Ernestine Yvonne Elam

    4. Frances Diana Elam

    4. Perry L. Elam

    4. Wanda Denise Elam

    4. David Lee Elam

    4. Duane Lee Elam

    4. Carolyn Delores Elam

    4. Herschell Walter Elam

    4. Cee Cee Marie Elam

Ida Mai passed away and Ernest married (2) Lucritia Price

+3. Willie George Elam married (1) Ida Christine Bonner and they had seventeen children:

    4. Willie George Elam, Jr.

    4. Walter Thomas Elam

    4. Mary Christine Elam

    4. Rowland Alonzo Elam

    4. Elizabeth Ann Elam

    4. James Franklin Elam

    4. Norman Lee Elam

    4. Nathaniel Lewis Elam

    4. Deborah Rene Elam

    4. Melvin Andrew Elam

    4. Alice Juanita Elam

    4. Shirley Lenora Elam

4. Carl Anthony Elam

4. Carla Annete Elam

4. Earl Dwight Elam

4. Glenda Lorraine Elam

4. Riley Terrance Elam

4. Timothy Bryan Outing

+3. Calvin Franklin Elam married Jeanette Johnson and they moved to Michigan. They had five children:

4. Tony Devan Elam

4. Bruce Anthony Elam

4. Calvin Franklin Elam, Jr.

4. Donald Lee Elam

4. Kathleen Jeannette Elam

Jeanette Elam passed away and Calvin married (2) Dorothy Jones. They had no children.

+3. Clara Mai Elam married Charlie Chester Battles, Jr. They moved to Pennsylvania. Clara Mai and Charlie Battles had seven children:

4. Mary Jane Battles

4. Charles Chester Battles III

4. Billie Vincent Battles

4. Janice Lee Battles

4. Carolyn Joyce Battles

4. Louis Nelson Battles

4. Glenn Aaron Battles

+3. Mary Christine Elam married Robert Lee Fox and they had one child:

4. Sherby Chinel Fox

+3. Freddie Glenn Elam married Betty Jewel O'Bannon from Chicago and they adopted a child:

4. Margarette "Pepper" Elam

+3. Jessie Ruth Elam married (1) Curtis Phillips and they have one child:

4. Kenneth McDale Phillips

Jessie Ruth Elam Phillips married (2) Howard Lawrence Whitaker.

+3. Paul Howard Elam married Mary Frances Phillips and they have six children:

4. Timothy Scott Elam

4. Felicia Annette Elam

4. Tracy Lynn Elam

4. Gary Lopez Elam

4. James Howard Elam

4. Marlin Eugene Elam

The Coulter – Gray – Northcutt Families

1. James "Jim" Coulter built the Park Hotel in Tullahoma, which later became the family home. He married Lula Hale and they had two children:

2. Mark Coulter (died young)

2. Lula C. Coulter married (1) James Gray and they had one child:

3. Peggie Ann Gray married Robert Mitchell Northcutt and they have two daughters and one grandson:

4. Angelia Northcutt

4. Michelle Northcutt

4. Robert Waymond Northcutt

Lula married (2) James "J. C." Miller. They had no children.

The Eppinger Family

1. Grant Eppinger married Helen Horner and they had five children:

+2. Wilbert Eppinger

+2. Monica Eppinger

2. Wilbert Eppinger, Jr.

2. Tennie Rochelle Eppinger

2. William Roshun Eppinger

+2. Wilbert Eppinger married (1) Koran Diane Hogan and they had two daughters:

      3. Cheryl R. Eppinger has one daughter:

            4. Ryan Anise Jones

      3. Monica D. Eppinger married Joe Jackson

Wilbert Eppinger married (2) Rhonda L. Lewis and they have three children:

      3. Wilbert Eppinger, Jr. married Shammara Jones

      3. Tennie Rochelle Eppinger

      3. William Roshun Eppinger

The Turner Family

1. Marshall Turner married Annie _____ and they had three children:

      +2. Melvin Thomas Turner, Sr.

      2. Gary Allen Turner

      2. Carmen Annette Turner Hall

+2. Melvin Thomas Turner, Sr. married Evelyn Watson and they have four children:

      +3. Takyah Turner

      3. Melvin Turner, Jr.

      3. Lydia Turner

      3. Timothy Turner

      +3. Takyah Turner married Christopher Battles and they have a son:

            4. Dante Battles

SOURCES

Sources for all articles:

1850 Federal Census of Coffee County, TN, Schedules 1, 2, and 3
1860 Federal Census of Coffee County, TN, Schedules 1, 2, and 3
1870 Federal Census of Coffee County, TN, Schedules 1, 2, and 3
1880 Federal Census of Coffee County, TN
"Coffee County from Arrowheads to Rockets" by Corinne Martinez
"Coffee County Loose Records" (microfilm)
"Coffee County, TN Wills, Vol. 1: 1833-1860, Bk. 1" WPA transcript 1936
"Coffee County, Then and Now" by Basil B. McMahan
"Family Tree Magazine," Dec. 2002, p. 66
"The Flood of Years" by Miss Christine Vaughan
"The Heritage of Coffee County, Tennessee 1936-2004, c2005
"History of Coffee County" by Leighton Ewell; Doak Printing Co., Manchester, TN, c1936
"Manchester Times," various editions
"Mighty Rough Times, I Tell You: Personal Accounts of Slavery in TN" narratives collected by Fisk University Students and WPA workers; edited by Andrea Sutcliffe
"The Negro in Tennessee, 1790-1865" by Caleb Perry Patterson
"The People's Paper" Saturday, July 7, 1860
"Put in Master's Pocket: Interstate slave trading and the black Appalachian Diaspora" by Wilma A. Dunaway http://members.aol.com/wadunaway/slavery.htm
"Slavery's End in Tennessee, 1861-1865" by John Cimprich
"Tennessee: A Guide to the State" http://newdeal.feri.org/guides/tnguide/ch10.htm
"Tullahoma: the Campaign for the Control of Middle Tennessee" by Michael R. Bradley
"With Fire and Blood: Life Behind Union Lines in Middle TN, 1863-1865" by Michael R. Bradley

"I had crossed the line. I was free; but there was no one to welcome me to the land of freedom. I was a stranger in a strange land."
~~Harriet Tubman

Personal Profiles

Edmonia Murray

Entrepreneur

Murray's Home Baking and Catering Service

Born in Manchester on June 19th, 1932, and delivered by midwives, Edmonia Hill's busy life began. Born to Virgie Lee and Joe Irvin Hill, she grew up with three sisters and two brothers. In 1948 Virgie and her baby son died in childbirth. Edmonia was 16.

When Edmonia was about 4 years old her father took a job in Boston, and packed up his family and moved. Edmonia remembers traveling in a big covered truck. Her mother was willing to move because she was able to take her chickens with them. They lived in Boston a couple of years while her dad worked in a horse barn caring for show horses before moving back to Coffee County. She has been here ever since.

Young Edmonia Baking for Thanksgiving

As a child Edmonia attended the Rosenwald School on Rye Street. The school was intended for black children in grades k-8th, but children were allowed to attend as early as 3 or 4 years of age. After 8th grade, Edmonia and her classmates went to Davidson Academy (another Rosenwald School) in Tullahoma for high school. The Coffee County School Board would not provide school busses for the black children to get to Tullahoma resulting in them having to find their own transportation. Many never made it to Davidson. Others had to pay 25 cents a day for bus fare to ride. Edmonia remembers often having to stand up and give her seat to a white person. When the blacks finally got their own bus it often broke down making it difficult, if not impossible, for the children to get to school. Many did not graduate.

Edmonia graduated from Davidson Academy in 1950 and went on to attend Philander Smith College in Little Rock, Arkansas (the first college west of the Mississippi to make education available to African Americans). She studied there for a time but because of the lack of funds had to leave and return home.

As a young girl, Edmonia took jobs babysitting and cleaning houses for various people. When she was about 11-12 years-old she was employed by the Mrs. Olive and Mr. Wright Hickerson, Sr. family. Here she would clean and do laundry, but she did not cook. She babysat for Mrs. Edith and Mr. Wright Hickerson, Jr. The Hickersons held parties and family dinners and it was here that she learned how to set a proper table and to serve. She would get so very nervous worrying about making a mistake. The Hickersons became like family to her.

Edmonia's mother had taught her how to cook, and when she went to work at Sanders' Café (which was located next to Lawson's Store) her cooking training expanded. She would cook from 6 a.m. to 6 p.m. for $12.00 a week.

Segregation existed but no one ever thought much about it. It's just the way things were. When she arrived at the Hickerson home to begin work the first day, she knocked on the side door. The door was answered but she was sent around to the back of the house to use the back door. Edmonia and her friends would go to Hugh Leming's Drug Store, where they could buy ice cream, but were not allowed to sit on the bench in the store.

When he was 11 years-old, James Edward Murray and his family moved here from Guntersville, AL to work on a farm. After school all the children would play in a field until their parents came for them. Eddie claimed Edmonia as his girl and would follow her around. Anytime she spoke to another boy, Eddie was quick to announce that Edmonia was his girlfriend. She would vehemently deny it and he would hang his head. He persisted.

"Eddie took me to the movies one day and I guess he expected me to pay my own way. Admission was 20 cents, and that was all he'd brought," remembers Edmonia. "We were upstairs at the theater and he found someone to borrow some money from, so we stayed." It wasn't really a date.

Eddie kept coming around and wouldn't give up. Then one day he asked her to marry him. She thought, "I guess the only way I'm going to get rid of him is to marry him." And she did. But she made him go ask her father for permission first. Her birthday is June 19th, but Edmonia didn't want to get married that day

Home from the Army 1955

so they chose June 23rd, 1951 for their wedding day. That way she would get two gifts. They got married at home with 2 or 3 friends in attendance and for their reception had Vanilla Wafers and Kool-Aid (no cake). Eddie was 19 years old and Edmonia 18. They remained married for 65 years. They had big, formal weddings and receptions for their 25th, 35th and 50th anniversaries where they renewed their vows. Edmonia had informed the preacher and their friends ahead of time what she was going to do, and when the preacher asked "Do you take Eddie to be your husband?" she didn't respond. There was a long silence as surprise and shock was shown on Eddie's face.

50th Wedding Anniversary
Orra Mae Northcutt and Edmonia & Eddie Murray

Manchester held an annual 4th of July event in celebration of Independence Day, but the blacks were not allowed to attend. "Uncle" Lindsley Brewer, former slave to Dr. J. E. Rodes, is credited with being the organizer of the first 4th of August Celebration, the answer to the whites 4th of July. Stands were set up where food was sold; everyone played ball and there was music and dancing. Blacks and whites joined together in this Celebration Day and it became a fun tradition in Manchester for many years.

In 1965 Nadene Farmer was the only caterer in town and she hired Edmonia to help her. Edmonia was not permitted to bake, but she washed dishes, cleaned and kept her children. She would go on catering jobs with Nadene and because Nadene didn't know how to set a table, that became Edmonia's job. At one time, Nadene's husband was in the hospital and Nadene called Edmonia and wanted her to finish a cake for her. It was already baked. Edmonia remembers decorating it with yellow roses. She could cook but had never baked so she started making cakes for family. Nadene and her husband eventually moved away, leaving Manchester without a caterer.

Edmonia called Dr. Clarence Farrar and found out that she wouldn't need a license to start a business but she would need a blood test. With that taken care of, Murray's Home Bakery and Catering Service was begun. The year was 1970. Many people helped her to get her business off the ground. Nadene Farmer gave her a punchbowl set and various appliances. Martha Duncan worked for the Manchester Times and wrote a story about Edmonia which truly helped her business. As Edmonia made money she put everything back into the business buying dishes, tablecloths, etc. Munsey's Photography Studio and Smoot's Flowers and Gifts helped her tremendously; Leroy Munsey took pictures of her cakes and decorations and made photo albums for her and Donnie

Edmonia displaying one of her cakes

Smoot provided her with candelabras and tablecloths.

Murray's Catering became so busy that Edmonia needed help. She hired Orra Mae Northcutt as her assistant, and she worked for her for 20 years. Edmonia's family was there to help, too. Her husband would load and unload for her and do anything else he could help with. The largest wedding Edmonia ever catered was for 1,200 people. With experience came many truths: #1 was to plan for more people than expected at any event. As a result, she never, ever ran out of cake. Also, the cakes should not only *look* good, but *taste* good also. Her biggest pet peeve is a wrinkled table cloth.

Edmonia & Edd[ie]

Edmonia semi-retired in 2016 but will occasionally do a little work from home.

The Murrays have a daughter, Cynthia, one granddaughter, Shauné, and 3 great-grandchildren.

Edmonia and Eddie sponsored the Bordeaux Jr. Pro football team in Nashville in 1985 for underprivileged children by purchasing uniforms for them.

Over the years Edmonia has served on many committees and organizations:

She was a member of the Eastern Star where she was crowned

President of Business & Professional Woman's Club

Soroptimist (helping women and children in the local community)

Coffee County Manchester Library Board

Hospital Auxiliary--Is currently the Hospitality Committee Chairman

Was a Notary for many years

Sunday School teacher

Served on Committee to build the Y.M.C.A.

Edmonia accepted Christ in 1947. She has been teaching Sunday School for the past 60 years at the Stephen's Chapel United Methodist Church. Of the many committees she has served on, working in her church (where she has served in many capacities) has been the most important to her.

Edmonia has always found it simple to love. "Life wasn't always easy. I worked hard but enjoyed it. I always tried to show love to the people around me, and to encourage them. God was good then, and He still is."

Edmonia in Retirement – January 2018
"God is Good."

Lonnie Norman

Mayor – City of Manchester

It was early in the springtime of 1941 that Jim (1902-1971) and Matilda Nevels (1906-1993) Norman were blessed with the birth of their first child, a son. Lonnie Norman made his entrance into this world on March 28th. Three other Norman children would follow: Oscar (1942-2009), Carl and Zeda Norman.

Matilda came from a large family in Hillsboro.

As a child, Norman and his friends enjoyed shooting marbles, playing softball and playing in the creek that is behind where Riverview School was built. He attended the Rosenwald School on Rye Street and later the Davidson Academy in Tullahoma. Busses would bring all students in from Summitville, Beech Grove and Hillsboro and there a bus would carry the older children to Tullahoma. He remembers that Ike Nevels drove the bus.

While in school, Lonnie enjoyed playing football. Although the black students could not attend school with the whites, they were allowed to play each other in sports. They would play on the College Street Campus after school and play sports with each other. Everyone was allowed to attend the football games; however, blacks were only allowed to sit in the end zone, where the bleachers were rotting and falling in. During one game Lonnie was injured. He'd been hit in the chest and was having trouble breathing. When the ambulance arrived, they informed Lonnie that the hospital in town refused to treat him, so he was taken to the hospital in Sewanee. Lonnie played football for the four years he was at Davidson Academy.

Lonnie graduated from Davidson and about three or four years later went to Trade School for a degree in electronics. When he applied for a job at Sverdrop Technology on the AEDC Base he had to bring in his diploma to prove he had graduated. The machinists didn't have to have graduated. He was first hired to work as a janitor (the title "laborer" would have paid ten cents an hour more). He was not allowed to eat in the cafeteria, but was able to work his way up to Lead Technician, then Supervisor.

As a youth Lonnie became close to J. D. Ring and his entire family. When he was about 10 or 12 years old, he began mowing yards and doing other odd jobs for the Rings. J. D.'s sister's son, Keith Lovelady, was a doctor. One time after cleaning out a brush row, Lonnie woke in the night with chest pains. He called Keith about 3:00-4:00 in the morning hoping to get him to call in something for the pain. Lonnie thought he had pulled a muscle. Because it was a heart issue Keith refused to prescribe anything and put him in the hospital instead. Tests were done and it was discovered Lonnie had a malignant tumor. Lymphoma. He underwent chemotherapy treatments Mondays through Fridays for six months until he was declared cancer-free. He continues today with regular follow-up checkups. Lonnie credits Keith with saving his life.

Sam's Place was a Café on Rye Street run by a Norman's cousin, Sam Nevels. It became a hangout for the local kids – a place where they could get a cold drink for five cents, if they had it. Lonnie could get a drink if his Momma would buy. More often Lonnie and his friends would go out collecting bottles that they could cash in for change to buy their drinks.

When he was about 18 years old, a friend of Lonnie's, J. D. Ring, lost his billfold and Lonnie found it. When J. D. was telling Lonnie about losing it, Lonnie played ignorance and asked it he'd had any money in it. "Yes. About $3,000" was the reply. "No. Actually, it was more than $3,000" was Lonnie's comeback and he returned the billfold. As Lonnie drove away in his beat-up old pick-up truck, J. D. remarked that "There goes an honest man. You can trust him with anything."

Highway 41 was the main road in town and to get there Lonnie would work his way around through the side streets, thus avoiding the whites who would pick on, and make fun of, him.

Times were hard when Lonnie was growing up, but everybody had it the same. He can't imagine what his grandfather and great-grandfather went through. He believes going through tough times makes a person better. Lonnie has never held any bitterness.

As a young man Lonnie always kept up with politics. When he turned 21, he registered to vote and has never missed participating in an election since. Gwyn Walker was Police Chief in 1984 and he told Lonnie that he should run for Alderman. He ran on the Democratic ticket, won, and served from 1984 to 1991. He then ran for Mayor where he served 1991 to 1995; then was Alderman again until 2012, and then Mayor again until now. He has always strived to make things better for his employees. In 1984 the Street Department had no offices. With Alvin West, an Alderman on the Steering Committee, they found a place, bought the land and a place was built for the Street Department.

Lonnie married Mildred Pryor in 1963 and they had four children: Virginia (1955-2004), Deborah, Priscilla and Lonnie, Jr., and two granddaughters: Brandi Sails (1982-2014) and Kandi Guest. Mildred passed away in 2016.

Today, kids can vote at 18. They should register to vote and never miss a chance to do so. A lot of people will run for public office for the wrong reasons. The title that is above his name on his door will disappear and his name will be what remains. Lonnie wants people to remember that he always did the best he could do. His advice to young people is to do the right thing. Never put anyone down but treat them as you would wish to be treated. And, listen to your parents. They know what they are talking about.

Lonnie currently has no plans for retirement.

Mayor Lonnie Norman
"Always treat others as you would want to be treated."

Lorene Hickerson McReynolds
Nonagenarian

Lorene Hickerson McReynolds' great-grandparents were Clarissa and Lawyer Robert Vannoy (see article "Vannoy Recalls Days of Slavery"), and her grandfather was their son, William Robert "Will" Vannoy.

Will Vannoy married Ella Brewer and they had six children, Eulah Beatrice Carrie Vannoy being the oldest and the mother of Lorene. Eulah married John Thomas Hickerson and they had seven children, Lorene

Will and Ella Brewer Vannoy (Lorene's grandparents), taken outside their home on Harp Street in Manchester.

being the next to youngest and the only one still living.

Lorene was born in Manchester on August 10, 1928 and attended the Rosenwald School in Manchester, then the Davidson Academy in Tullahoma. She began working at Modernistic Beauty Shop when she was 12-years-old and continued working there through her high school graduation. She had numerous jobs where she ran errands, including making runs to the bank and to the post office. After graduation from Davidson Academy she went on to graduate in 1949 from Tennessee Agricultural & Industrial State College. Her first job was at Wilberforce University in Ohio, working in the Veterans Office. James McReynolds from Russellville, KY was attending college there and it was here that they met. Lorene and James were married in 1953. Her next job was at

Wright-Patterson Air Force Base in Dayton, Ohio, where she was employed as a Supply Requirements and Distributions Officer in publishing.

Lorene and James had two children: James, Jr. and Joni. James graduated from the United States Air Force Academy and remained in the Air Force until he retired as a Lieutenant Colonel. He met his wife, Dorothy, in Denver and they have two daughters, Amber and Lindsay. They are currently living in Yorktown, VA.

Joni McReynolds, like her mother, graduated from Tennessee State University. She worked as a flight attendant and later obtained a job with the Federal Government in Washington, D.C. She retired 20 years later after a very successful career with the government.

Lorene's parents:
John Thomas & Eulah Vannoy Hickerson

Lorene lived in Ohio for more than 30 years. After the passing of her husband James in 1977, Lorene moved back home to Manchester. Since her old house burned down, she built her present home on the same lot that she grew up on.

Lorene loves to travel and has done so extensively. When her daughter, Joni did her college student teaching in Mexico City, Lorene put her on a plane and she left the airport with a ticket for her first trip to Mexico City in hand. She has traveled all over the world. Her longest trips have been to Australia and China. On one trip, she flew from California to Hong Kong and cruised to several countries in Asia. On one trip she flew to Sydney, Australia, with stopovers in California and Hawaii. Among the other places she has visited include: Rome, the Vatican, London, Paris, Holland, Jamaica, Hong Kong, Singapore, Philippines, and Thailand, just to name a few.

Her children had been stationed in Germany, separately, for three years each, so for six years she made annual sojourns to Germany.

Lorene's favorite mode of traveling is on cruise ships. She loves cruising! Her last cruise was to Alaska. One year, 70 family members went on a cruise together to the Caribbean Islands. The next cruise she has planned will be with her daughter. They will cruise to the Caribbean again, this time stopping to spend a day in Cuba.

Lorene has always managed to stay busy. She enjoys reading, sewing and working jigsaw puzzles. She is a member of the South Central Tennessee Chapter of the Tennessee State University Alumni Association, a member of the

Hospital Auxiliary, and a member of the Main Street Church of Christ. She has worked with the Bible Correspondence at the Main Street Church of Christ since 1979.

Lorene Hickerson McReynolds
February 2019 – 90-years old

Her advice to young people: "Enjoy Life. Get a taste of everything. Do things. Discover what you like and what you want to do."

INDEX

(The names with a 0 in front are slaves)

Bailey, Julia, 84
Baily, J. R., 40
Baily, Jesse, 67
Baily, John R., 31
Baine, Andrew, 30
Baker, Alfred, 17
Baker, Charles, 41
Baker, Infant, 18
Baker, Molly, 17
Baker, Priscilla, 17
Baker, Reuben, 17
Baptist, 62
Barner, Charles, 67
Barnes, William, 67
Barton, Abner, 31, 41
Barton, Angelina, 16
Barton, Benjamin, 31
Barton, Martin, 41
Bashaw, J. E., 41
Bashaw, Joseph, 31
Batie, John, 67
Battles Family, 115, 118
Battles, Billie Vincent, 118
Battles, Carolyn Joyce, 118
Battles, Charles Chester III, 118
Battles, Charlie Chester, Jr., 118
Battles, Christopher, 120
Battles, Clara Mai Elam, 118
Battles, Dante, 120
Battles, Glenn Aaron, 118
Battles, Janice Lee, 118
Battles, Louis Nelson, 118
Battles, Mary Jane, 118
Battles, Takyah Turner, 120
Baugh Family, 115, 116
Baugh, Georgia Scrubbs, 116
Baugh, Gilbert, 88
Baugh, Gladys Willis, 116
Baugh, Willis, 15, 88, 116
Beachharg, B. N., 41
Beaty, Anthony, 67, 95
Becket, Andrew, 94
Bedford County, 62
Beech Grove, 110, 130
Beel, John, 27
Bell, William, 67
Berry, Henry, 93
Berry, J. W., 41
Berry, Sanford, 20
Berry, William, 20
Bible Correspondence, 136
Biddle, Eliza, 67
Biles Family, 115

Biles, Lydia, 59
Bill of civil rights, 64
Bird, Samuel, 31
Bishop, Sam, 67
Black sailors, 51
Black Schools, 60
Black soldiers, 51
Black, Alfred, 86
Blackburn, J. H., 41
Blair, Eleanor, 25
Blair, James, 81
Blair, Mary, 87
Blair, Milley, 81
Blair, Nathan, 67
Blair, R. D., 31
Blair, Samuel, 67
Blair, Thomas, 25
Blanton, John, 67
Blanton, Newton, 31
Blanton, Smith, 32
Blanton, Thadeus, 95
Blanton, Thadious, 67
Blanton, Wilkins, 41
Blanton, Willis, 32, 41
Bobo, Susy, 67
Boman, Green, 101
Boney, Adeline, 95
Bonner, Chas, 92
Bonner, Ida Christine, 117
Bonner, Jane, 103
Bonner, Jane Elam, 116
Bonner, William, 92
Bordeaux Jr. Pro football team, 128
Bough, George, 67
Bounds, Wesley, 85
Bowden, Elaine, 67
Bowden, F. W., 26
Bowden, G. E., 41
Bowden, G. L., 23
Bowden, Nancy, 23
Bowden, William, 23
Bowdon, G. E., 32
Bowen, Adaline, 67
Bowen, Frank, 67, 88
Bowls, Pleasant, 88
Bowman, Rufus, 87
Bowman, Thomas, 96
Boyd, F. M., 32
Bradley, Michael, 58
Brannon, Pinkney, 55
Brantley, James A., 32, 41
Brawley, C. C., 41
Brenn, Rhodes, 67

Fults, George, 87
Ganaway, Alice, 70
Garrett, Delila, 70
Garrison, Mike, 61
Gather, Rebecca, 33
Gaunt, Steven, 96
Gearneky, Thomas, 70
George, Maxwell, 83
Germany, 136
Gibson, William B., 33
Gilliam, David, 70
Gilliam, Joseph, 90
Gilliam, Rose, 92
Gordon, Rev., 108
Gotcher, Jesse, 33
Grant, Lere, 70
Gray Family, 119
Gray, George, 70
Gray, James, 119
Gray, Lula C. Coulter, 119
Gray, Peggie Ann, 119
Green Meadow Church of Christ, 62
Green, James, 34
Green, John, 71
Green, Mary, 43
Green, R. H., 43
Green, Washington, 71
Greenville, Tennessee, 52
Grer, Walter, 101
Gross, Joseph, 88
Guest Family, 115
Guest, Kandi, 132
Guinn, Margaret Davidson, 23
Gunn, Anderson, 89
Gunn, Druzilla, 87
Gunn, Hannah, 71
Gunn, Jane, 91
Gunn, Michael, 34
Gunn, T. L., 43
Gunn, Thomas L., 34
Guntersville, AL, 125
Gwinn, Rance, 100
Gwinn, William, 71
Gwyn, Thomas, 96
Gwynn, John, 88
Gwynn, Rance, 100, 101, 102
Gwynn, William, 71
Haggard, Robert M., 34
Haggerty, Judy, 30
Haggerty, Peter, 30
Hagins, Clara, 34
Hagis, Claig, 30
Haig, James, 71

Hale, Andrew, 71
Hale, Andy, 96
Hale, David, 71
Hale, Houston, 85
Hale, Luke, 85
Hale, Lula, 119
Hale, Solomon, 96
Hale, Sydney, 43
Hall, Carmen Annette Turner, 120
Hall, Cherry, 94
Hall, Elizabeth, 71
Hall, G. W., 59
Hall, James W., 43
Hall, William, 71, 82
Halpin, Jaw, 30
Ham, Norman J., 34
Hamilton, Elijah, 84
Hamins, Matthew, 71
Hammins, Arington, 88
Hammins, Arrington, 71
Hampton Mill, 13
Hampton, Aaron, 92
Hampton, Ransom, 34
Hampton, Ransome, 43
Hancock, M. L., 43
Hancock, Martin, 34
Hancock, Mary, 39
Hancock, Samuel, 37
Hanley, Alfred, 71
Hanly, Alf, 93
Harbin, Sampson, 9
Hardaway, Benjamin F., 34
Harden, Abner, 93
Hardin, Oliver, 71
Harp place, 21
Harp, Esther, 71
Harpe, Celia, 34
Harris, 27
Harris, A. H., 60
Harris, Ben, 12
Harris, Drunell, 92
Harris, Emily, 90
Harris, Henry, 84
Harris, Lettie, 92
Harris, Lewis, 34, 43
Harris, Mr., 58
Harris, Sinai Cunningham, 25
Harris, William, 43
Harrison, Nancy, 21
Harrison, P., 22
Harrison, Raybon, 71
Harrison, Thomas, 21
Hart, Moses, 43

148

Norton, H. C., 13
Norton, Henderson, 74
Norton, Henry W., 36, 46
Norton, Henry Wilson, 36
Norton, J. K., 46
Norton, Lucinda, 74
Norton, Margaret, 74
Norton, Moriah, 82
Norton, N. G., 46
Norton, N. P., 36, 46
Norton, Norman, 36
Norton, Norman G., 36
Norton, R. J., 46
Norton, Rufus, 46
Norton, William S., 36
Norton, Wilson, 22
Norton, Wm., 46
Nortons, 27
Norvill, Pharoh, 85
Norville, Cisero, 83
Notary, 128
Oaf, Julia, 74
Oaks, James, 21
Oats, Julia, 55
O'Bannon, Betty Jewel, 118
Ogleby, Dinah, 75
Old Uncle Ned, 102
Old West, 99
Oldham, Cherry, 94
Oldham, George, 94
Oliver, John, 90
Olum, Zo, 75
Ordman, Zarey, 55
Osborn, Barkly, 82
Osborne, Horace, 109, 110, 111
Osborne, Joseph, 97
Osburn, Lavinia, 75
Oscal, Adam, 75
Outing, Timothy Bryan, 118
Owens, Ab, 83
Owensboro, KY, 102
Paris, 135
Park Hotel, 119
Parkinson, Alfred, 75
Parmer, Fitz, 9
Parson, J. E., 46
Parson, Solomon, 47
Parten, Hannah King, 21
Paskett, Bob, 75
Paten, Margaret, 75
Patten, Andrew, 75
Patten, Henry, 75
Patten, John, 75

Patterson Place, 11
Patterson, John, 92
Patterson, Thomas, 94
Patton Chapel Church, 100
Patton daughters, 62
Patton, Andrew, 75
Patton, Andy, 82
Patton, Ben, 11, 62, 63
Patton, Benjamin, 75, 91
Patton, Harrison, 91
Patton, Henry, 75, 84
Patton, Isaac, 75, 91
Patton, J. J., 7
Patton, James, 75
Patton, Jeff, 75
Patton, John, 36, 75
Patton, John J., 47
Patton, Joseph, 36, 47
Patton, Lavina, 75
Patton, Lewis, 75
Patton, Maranda, 75
Patton, Mariah, 75, 91
Patton, Mary, 75
Patton, Mirandy, 91
Patton, Thomas, 91
Patton, Victoria, 91
Patton's Chapel School, 60
Payne, Haney, 18
Payne, J. S., 47
Pearson, Adaline, 75
Pearson, Henry, 75, 92
Pearson, J. E., 46
Pearson, Maggie, 88
Peay, Mariah, "Aunt", 14
Pennibarker, Mr., 55
Penson, Lydia, 19
Penson, W. F., 47
Pepper, Henry, 96
Perkins, Cory, 87
Perkins, Frances, 91
Perkins, Jack, 75
Perkins, Tereace, 75
Person, Solomon, 47
Petty, Mary, 75, 94
Petty, R. M., 47
Petty, Sallie, 93
Petty, Sarah, 75
Philander Smith College, 124
Philippines, 135
Philips, Jack, 75
Philips, James, 36
Philips, Lorenzo, 36
Philips, Micajah, 36

Philips, Sarah, 36
Philips, William, 36
Phillips, Curtis, 118
Phillips, Jessie Ruth Elam, 118
Phillips, Johnathan, 26
Phillips, Kenneth McDale, 119
Phillips, Lorenzo D., 47
Phillips, M. C., 47
Phillips, Mary Frances, 119
Phillips, Sarah, 26, 47
Phillips, Shack, 89
Phillips, W. H., 47
Phillips, Wm., 47
Pinkard, David, 82
Pinkard, James, 84
Pinkard, Maggie, 12, 13
Pinson, Cleo, 18
Pinson, Gun, 18
Pinson, Margaret, 18
Pirtle, Robert, 36
Pittman, J. E., 47
Poindexter, Amanda, 37
Politto, Mattie, 60
Polk, James K., 5
Poor House, 55
Powell, Alex, 47
Powell, Alexander, 37
Powell, D. J., 47
Powell, W. D., 47
Powers, Charles, 75, 83
Powers, Francis, 76
Powers, Henry, 37
Powers, John H., 37
Powers, Moses, 76, 83
Powers, Samuel, 76
Powers, Thomas, 37, 40, 47
Powers, Vence, 76
Powers, William, 47
Prairie Plains, 60, 62, 63, 100
Pratt, Jim, 107
Preston, John, 76
Price, Emily, 76
Price, Isaac, 18
Price, John, 76
Price, Joseph, 18
Price, Lucritia, 117
Price, Mary, 18
Price, P. H., 47
Price, Peter, 18
Price, Pleasant H., 37
Price, Porter, 108
Price, R. J., 47
Price, Reuben, 37

Price, Richard, 37
Price, Sam, 76
Price, Samuel, 76
Price, Wesley, 89
Price, Winny, 18
Prince, Andrew, 76
Pruitt, Isaac, 76
Pruitt, Rose, 76
Pruitt, Thomas, 76
Pryor, Mildred, 132
Pryor, W. A., Rev., 62
Puckett, E. B., 47
Pulaski, Tenn., 56
Pulley, Gideon, 47
Pulley, W. H., 47
Pully, Gideon, 37
Putnam, W. W., 47
Pyson, J. C., 47
Raburn, George, 17
Raburn, Mary, 37
Ragan, Susan, 47
Ragsdale, Mariah, 76
Ramsey Family, 115
Ramsey, A. J., 47
Ramsey, Annah, 76
Ramsey, Carroll, 76
Ramsey, Nelson, 87
Ramsey, Peter, 82
Ramsey, Sammie Mae, 57
Ramsey, William, 76
Ramsey, Willis, 96
Randall, David, 47
Rankin, Douglas, 94
Rankin, John, 37
Rankins, John, 47
Raven Street, 61
Ray, Charles, 9
Ray, Eva, 9
Ray, George McGuff, 9
Ray, Margaret, 9
Ray, Robert, 9, 96
Ray, Willis, 9
Rayborn, Jennie, 76
Rayburn, Adam, 26
Rayburn, French, 47
Rayburn, J. W. G., 47
Rayburn, James, 47
Rayburn, Lewis, 83
Rayburn, Oten, 82
Rayburn, R. D., 48
Rayburn, Robert S., 24
Rayburn, Sarah, 26, 37
Rayburn, W. K., 48

158

40710843R00091

Made in the USA
Middletown, DE
30 March 2019